Reading Highlights

Jacob Murray

2

WorldCom Edu

Reading Highlights

CONTENTS

On the cover
When a giant molasses tank burst in downtown Boston, nobody was prepared for the deadly mess that followed. **page 65**

Normal sports aren't exciting enough for you? Then try extreme ironing. The top of a mountain is only one spot where people participate in this strange sport. **page 41**

Folktale

Old stories of ghosts and strange beings are hard to believe, but they aren't always just fiction.

Light

Light gives us life and shows us the world. But it can be used for so much more.

Trees

Trees can give life, but they can also take it away. Learn how some trees are more than they seem.

Competition

Whether you play to win, or just for fun, games are great entertainment for people across the world.

Unsolved Mysteries

Will she ever die? Who was he really? Perhaps you can answer these questions after reading the two intriguing stories here.

I low did all the dinosaurs die? No one knows exactly, but scientists have some pretty good ideas. **page 71**

How a fungus takes control of carpenter ants? **page 77**

Sign outside Woolpit
The village sign for Woolpit, England depicts two green children and a wolf. This picture represents a story that goes back to the 12th century.

01 UNIT From Fiction to Fact

Guesswork

Discuss your answers to these questions with your classmates.

1. Can you imagine what the Woolpit legend is about?
2. Do you think the Woolpit legend is funny or scary?
3. Why do you think the children are green?

MP3

▲ **Pit for hunting wolves**
Some people think that Woolpit got its name from a wolf pit nearby.

From Fiction to Fact

An old folk tale tells of two green-skinned children, a boy and a girl, who mysteriously appeared in Woolpit, England. Villagers discovered them in old pits that were designed to trap wolves. The children were confused and starving, and couldn't speak a word of English.

The kind village people took the children in and cared for them. At first they would only eat green beans, and soon the boy died. The girl learned to eat other food, and her skin lost its green color. She eventually learned to speak English. Then she finally told her fantastic story.

▲ **St. Mary's Church, Bury St. Edmunds**
According to Harris's theory, the children were hiding out in Thetford forest when they heard the church bells of Bury St. Edmunds. The sound led them through underground passages to Woolpit.

The girl said she came from St. Martin's Land, an underground world where everybody was green! Some took this as a sign that the children were fairies, or even aliens. Historian Paul Harris doesn't believe this, but he does think the girl was telling the truth—or at least her version of it.

Harris says the children probably came from a Flemish village named Fornham St. Martin, which was about 8 miles from Woolpit. He thinks the children were orphans who ran away after their parents died. He suggests that they survived in the forest by eating vegetables, and then later wandered into an old mine shaft. They walked through the dark mine and eventually came out near Woolpit.

The girl's story of an underground world? It was how she remembered the mine shaft. And the children's green skin? Harris says that it came from their poor diet of forest vegetables.

Vocabulary

A. Circle the correct answer and write it in the blank.

		a.	b.
1.	A folk tale is a kind of ________.	**a.** performance	**b.** story
2.	A pit is a kind of ________.	**a.** deep hole	**b.** thick forest
3.	To be confused is to ________.	**a.** not know	**b.** believe
4.	A starving person should be given ________.	**a.** water	**b.** food
5.	A green bean is a long, green ________.	**a.** leaf	**b.** vegetable
6.	Fairies are ________ creatures.	**a.** imaginary	**b.** real
7.	Orphans are children without ________.	**a.** food	**b.** parents
8.	A historian studies the ________.	**a.** past	**b.** future
9.	Your diet is the ________.	**a.** food you eat	**b.** clothes you wear
10.	To wander is to move without ________.	**a.** thinking	**b.** walking

B. Draw lines to match the expressions with their opposites.

1.	care for •	• lie
2.	tell the truth •	• go back
3.	run away •	• harm

Reading Comprehension

A. Main Ideas. Complete the statement by circling the correct choice for each blank.

The passage is mainly about the **1.** __________ of **2.** __________ . So the main idea is that **3.** __________ .

1. a. truth　　b. diet

2. a. the villagers　　b. an old fairy tale

3. a. there is an explanation for the story of the green-skinned children of Woolpit
b. the poor diet of the children caused their skin to turn green

B. Details. Complete the sentences by circling the correct answer.

1. Paul Harris thinks that __________ .

a. the girl was lying about her story
b. there is some truth in the girl's fantastic story
c. the girl really came from an underground world where everybody was green

2. The children ran away to the forest because __________ .

a. they had no one to care for them
b. they wanted to find the old mine shaft
c. their parents said they were going to die

C. Inferences. Read each statement and decide if you think it is likely or unlikely. Check the appropriate box.

	Likely	Unlikely
1. The boy died because of his poor diet.	☐	☐
2. The villagers of Woolpit often went to Fornham St. Martin.	☐	☐
3. The children were brother and sister.	☐	☐
4. The girl believed she was telling the truth about what happened.	☐	☐

Writing

A. Organize. Number the events in the correct order from 1-5.

B. Synthesize. Using Organize above, fill in the blanks in the "Lost Children" poster.

Who: two young children

Last Seen: near the edge of the forest

The children's parents __________ and they ran away into the __________. We are worried that they won't be able to survive on their own, or that they may wander into an __________ __________ __________. If you have any information regarding these children's whereabouts, please contact us as soon as possible.

02 UNIT

Real Enough

The Flying Dutchman by Albert Pinkham Ryder c.1887 (Smithsonian American Art Museum): The legend of the Flying Dutchman concerns a ghost ship that can never make port, doomed to sail the oceans forever. It probably originates in 17th century folklore.

Guesswork

Discuss your answers to these questions with your classmates.

1. Describe this painting. Can you see the people in the boat?
2. What will happen to the people in the boat?
3. What are they afraid of?

RH2-02
MP3

Real Enough

It is a sailor's worst nightmare. The weather is calm and the wind is still, when suddenly a ship is spied on the horizon. As it gets closer, the sailor becomes frightened. The ship is moving, but there is no wind! It's the Flying Dutchman!

The legend of the Flying Dutchman starts in 1614. A Dutch ship was trying to make it around the Cape of Good Hope when it sank. As the legend goes, the captain mistakenly sailed his ship into a terrible storm. He and his crew fought for hours to sail the ship back to safety. Eventually, it crashed into some rocks and began to sink. Just before they went under, the captain screamed out a curse: "I WILL round this Cape even if I have to keep sailing until the end of time!" Sailors say that to this day his ghost is still trying to sail around the Cape!

Every sailor who traveled the African coast knew that seeing the Flying Dutchman was a bad omen. But there are worse things than bad luck. Sometimes the dead crew of the Dutchman would ask sailors to carry messages for them: messages addressed to people who were long dead. Any sailor foolish enough to accept one was doomed to die soon.

No one knows if the Flying Dutchman was real or just a story. But that may not matter. It was real enough in the minds of the sailors who think they saw her.

◀ Willem van der Decken, captain of the Flying Dutchman: One tale of the Flying Dutchman claims the captain sold his soul to the devil and now he is doomed to sail the seas forever.

◀ Prince George of Wales, later King George V of England, reported seeing the Flying Dutchman in his youth. He described it as glowing with a strange red light. Shortly after the sighting, a sailor fell from high on the ship and died.

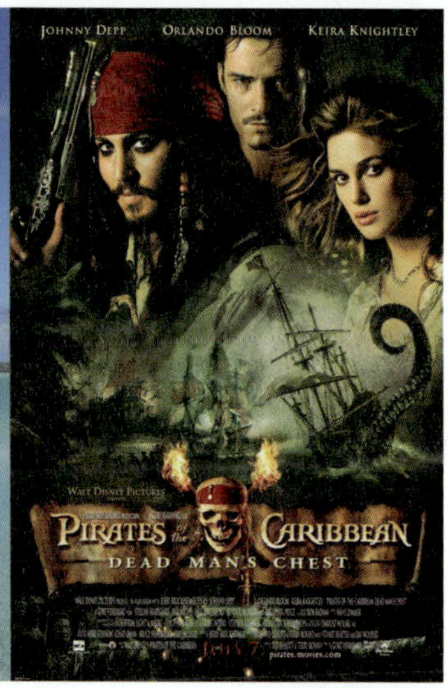

◀ The Flying Dutchman appeared as a ghost ship in the movie, Pirates of the Caribbean.

▲ The Cape of Good Hope; looking towards the west, from the coastal cliffs above Cape Point

Vocabulary

A. Circle the answer that fits best with the word in red.

1. **nightmare** dream / story / tale
2. **sailor** earth / ocean / sky
3. **frightened** excited / scared / curious
4. **crew** audience / workers / athletes
5. **scream** mouth / eyes / nose
6. **accept** take / give / remove
7. **omen** sign / statue / building
8. **captain** follower / maker / leader
9. **foolish** silly / smart / clever
10. **spy** hear / see / smell

B. Draw lines to make correct sentences. Write the completed sentences below.

1. Our boat •	• hit a rock and we swam away •	• on the horizon.
2. We'll have to •	• saw a ghostly looking ship •	• to make it past the island.
3. They •	• row harder if we want •	• after it went under.

(1) Our boat ______________________________

(2) We'll have to ______________________________

(3) They ______________________________

Reading Comprehension

A. Main Ideas. Circle the answer that best completes each statement.

1. This story is about ________ .
   a. a ghost ship   b. a ghostly captain

2. Sailors were afraid of the Flying Dutchman because it was ________ .
   a. an old story   b. bad luck

3. According to the legend, the Flying Dutchman sank ________ .
   a. because it hit some rocks   b. because of the captain's curse

B. Details. Write True or False or Not Given after each statement.

1. Many sailors think that the Flying Dutchman is bad luck. ________
2. In 1614 a Dutch ship sank after it was caught in a terrible storm. ________
3. The Dutch ship was carrying gold around the Cape of Good Hope. ________
4. The crew caused the ship to sail into the storm. ________
5. The Flying Dutchman doesn't need wind to move. ________
6. Sometimes sailors would ask the crew of the Dutchman to carry messages. ________

C. Inferences. Decide which of the statements can be inferred from the passage. Check the correct answers. (Choose two.)

______ **1.** The tale of the Flying Dutchman has been around for a long time.

______ **2.** The captain of the Dutch ship was known for making terrible mistakes.

______ **3.** The crew cursed the captain for sailing them into the storm.

______ **4.** Sailors thought that the crew of the Dutchman were ghosts.

Writing

A. Organize. Place each detail in the correct box.

a. The Flying Dutchman sails without wind.
b. In 1614, a Dutch ship sank off the Cape of Good Hope.
c. Many Sailors think seeing the Dutchman is bad luck.
d. If you accept a message from the Flying Dutchman, you will die soon.
e. The captain screamed a curse as his ship sank.
f. Sailors claim the Flying Dutchman is still trying to sail around the cape.

Legend	Fact

B. Synthesize. Using Organize above, fill in the blanks in the advertisement for the play, The Flying Dutchman.

The Flying Dutchman

In ________ , a ________ ship ________ off the Cape of Good Hope.
Was that the end for the captain and his crew?
Or was it just the beginning?
Legend says that now the Flying Dutchman sails without ________ .
________ claim it is still trying to ________ around the Cape of Good Hope.
Seeing the Dutchman is ________ ________ .
But seeing its story isn't, so come enjoy the play!

03 UNIT

A Bright Idea

Guesswork

Discuss your answers to these questions with your classmates.

1. What are these people doing?
2. Does that water look safe to drink?
3. How could they clean that water?

▲ People in Sudan are learning how to use new solar cookers. The solar cooker is especially useful in Africa, where fuel is scarce but sunlight is plentiful.

▲ Solar oven (top) and solar panel cooker (bottom)

RH2-03
MP3

A Bright Idea

Did You Know?
Solar cookers can be built into the side of your house. All you need is a clear glass wall and a dark colored pot!

You are stranded in a blazing hot and sunny desert. You are dying of thirst and you've finally found water! But wait, the water is in a pool that many animals drink from. It could make you sick. How do you pasteurize it? You could use heat to kill the bacteria, but there is no wood or anything else to make a fire with. So what can you use to heat and clean the water? Give up? The sun!

All you need is some cardboard, tinfoil, a plastic bag and a pot. Shape the cardboard into a giant bowl, and

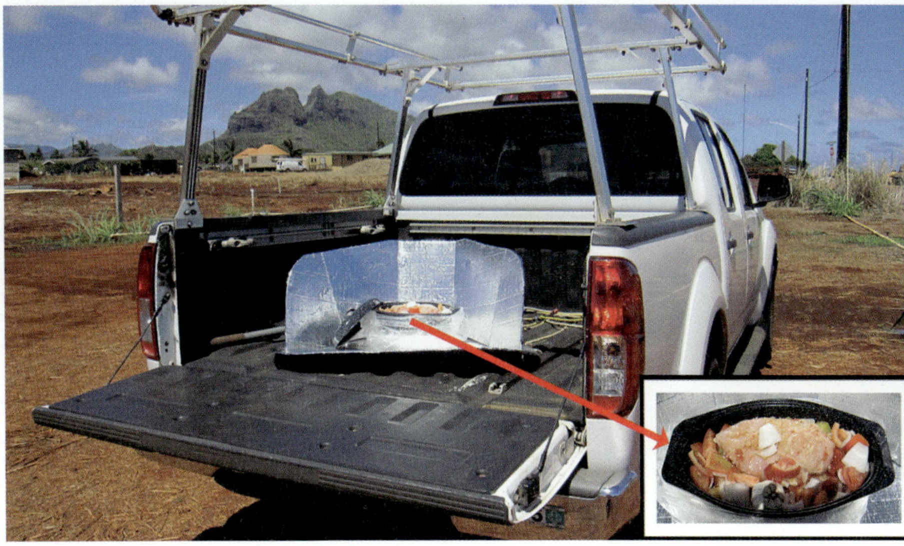

▲ Food cooks best in a solar cooker in the two hours before and after noon.

▲ Before and after pictures of a chicken and veggies dish made in a solar cooker

cover the inside with tinfoil. Fill the pot with water, tie the bag around it, and place it in the middle of the tinfoil-covered bowl. Leave the whole thing in direct sunlight for about 30 minutes. Then, take the pot out of the bag, but be careful, it will be hot. Your water will be safe to drink.

This isn't just an interesting experiment. This simple technology could save millions of lives. Nearly two million children die from drinking contaminated water every year. They get diarrhea from bacteria in the water. The diarrhea dehydrates and eventually kills the children. That solar cooker, which can be made from cheap, easy to find materials, kills those deadly bacteria. It can even be used to cook simple dishes. It's strange, but in the desert, the sun can be your best friend.

Vocabulary

A. Circle the correct answer and write it in the blank.

1. If something is blazing it is ________. **a.** cold **b.** hot

2. To pasteurize is to ________. **a.** clean **b.** collect

3. Bacteria are tiny ________. **a.** creatures **b.** products

4. Cardboard is made from ________. **a.** trees **b.** metal

5. A pot is used for ________. **a.** shaping **b.** cooking

6. Nearly means ________. **a.** nearby **b.** almost

7. To be contaminated is to be ________. **a.** dirty **b.** precious

8. Diarrhea comes from your ________. **a.** mouth **b.** bottom

9. To dehydrate is to lose ________. **a.** water **b.** energy

10. Deadly weapons are used to ________. **a.** hurt **b.** kill

B. Complete the sentences by choosing the correct answer.

1. I can make a fire ________.

a. to cook the food **b.** with the food

2. Don't give up yet! You still ________.

a. will fail **b.** might win

3. I don't want to live in the middle of town. ________.

a. I'd rather live on the outside **b.** I'd rather live in the center

Reading Comprehension

A. Main Ideas. Complete the statement by circling the correct choice for each blank.

The passage is mainly about the **1.**__________ of **2.**__________. So the main idea is that **3.**__________.

1. a. design and use b. shape and size

2. a. contaminated water b. a simple invention

3. a. cardboard, tinfoil, and a pot can be used to clean contaminated water
b. new inventions can be used to change clean water into contaminated water

B. Details. Circle the correct answer for each question.

1. Why is it important to pasteurize water?

a. because dirty water can make you sick
b. because sick people make dirty water
c. because the solar cooker cleans dirty water

2. How does the solar cooker pasteurize water?

a. it uses fire to heat the water
b. it changes the water with tinfoil
c. it heats the water with sunlight

C. Inferences. Decide which of the statements can be inferred from the passage. Check the correct answers. (Choose two.)

______ **1.** The solar cooker would not work without the tinfoil.

______ **2.** The solar cooker is more useful in places with a lot of sunlight.

______ **3.** Millions of solar cookers have saved lives all over the world.

______ **4.** The solar cooker can be used to make pizza and french fries.

Writing

A. Organize. Place each detail in the correct box.

a. shape cardboard into a large bowl
b. cover the cardboard with tinfoil
c. can be used anywhere the sun is shining
d. pasteurizes water
e. fill a pot with water and place it in a plastic bag
f. cheap and easy to make

The Solar Cooker	
How it's made	**How it's useful**

B. Synthesize. Using Organize above, complete the instructions for making a solar cooker, then match the each picture to the correct step of the instructions.

Build and use your own solar cooker!

1. Find some ________ and shape it into a large ________.
2. Cover the inside with ________.
3. Find a ________, and fill it with water. Place the pot in a plastic ________.
4. Place the pot in the tinfoil-covered cardboard ________.
5. Place the whole thing in direct ________. Wait.

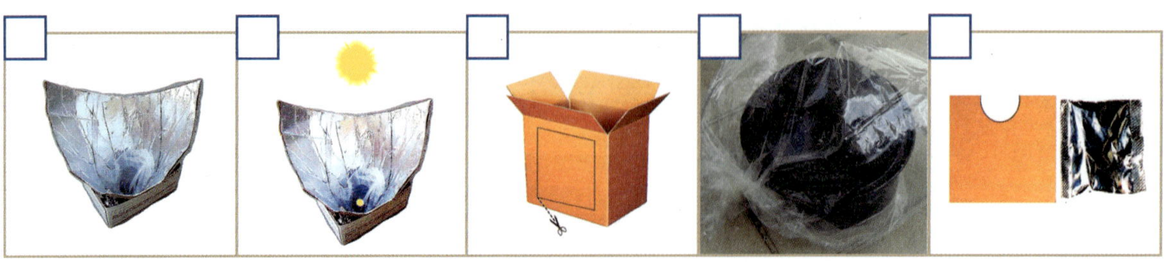

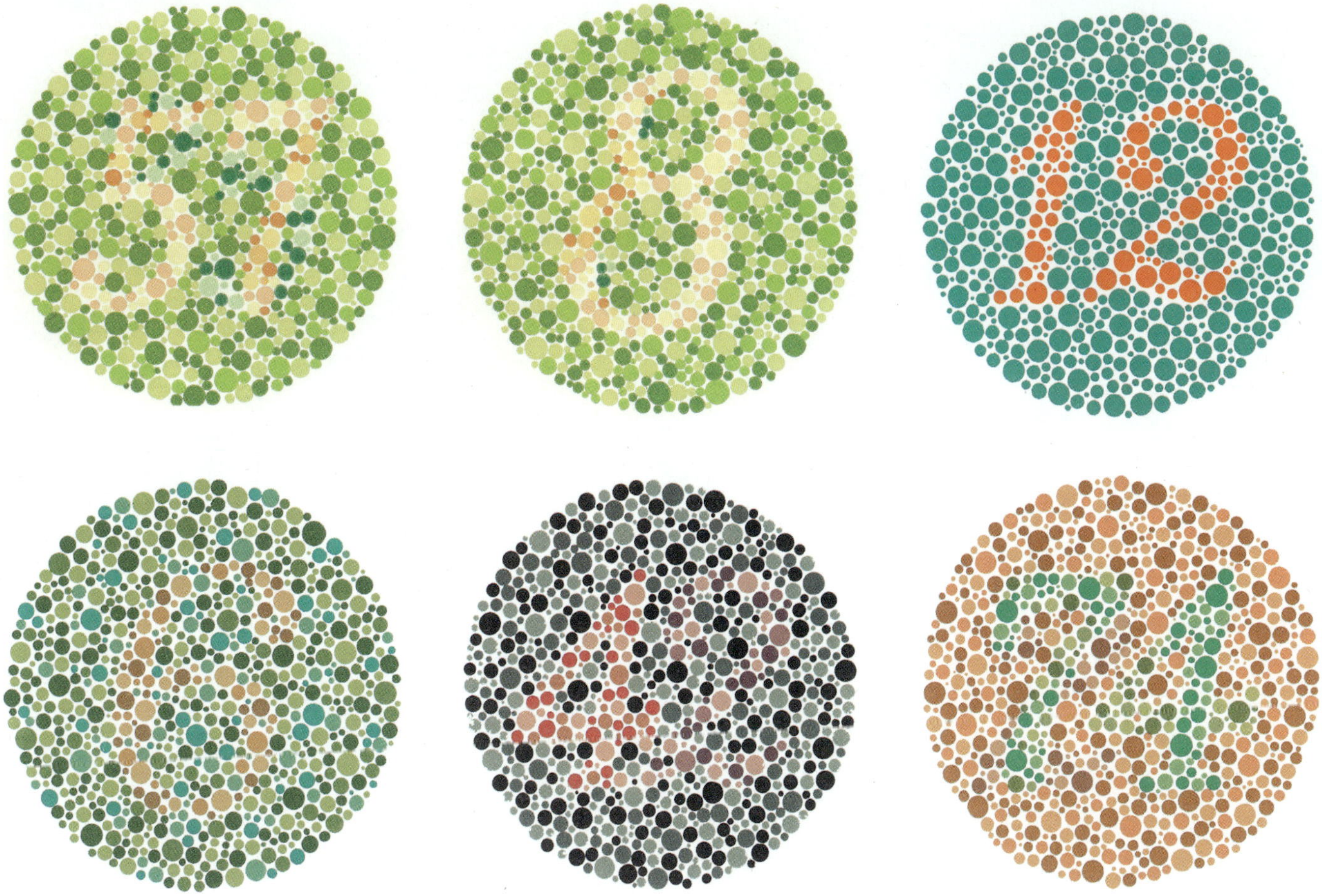

04 UNIT What Do You See?

Guesswork

Discuss your answers to these questions with your classmates.

1. Can you see all the numbers? Ask your classmates if they can see them as well.
2. Do you think every person sees these pictures the same way?
3. How do you think animals see these pictures?

RH2-04
MP3

What Do You See?

A hawk circles high up in the sky. Suddenly it dives to the ground. It reaches out and catches a small mouse in its talons, and then flies back up into the sky. How did it know exactly where that tiny mouse was? Well, for one thing, it has incredible long-distance vision. But that's not all. Hawks can see colors that humans can't!

Color is the way that our brains see different kinds of light. When light hits something, the light bounces back into our eyes. It bounces off of different things in different ways. Our brain sees these differences as colors. This is why an apple looks red and grass looks green. The ability to see color is very important because it allows creatures to identify food, and to easily tell different things apart.

Our brains can see three main colors; red, green, and blue. Each unique color is made up of different combinations and shades of these three. Dogs and some other kinds of mammals see two main colors, blue and yellow. Many marine animals can only see one. Most birds, on the other hand, can see four main types of color!

An important color that birds can see is called ultraviolet light. We know it is there because we can detect it with machines. Birds don't need machines, though. They see it in the trails of rodents, like mice, and on other birds. It's impossible to imagine exactly how they see the world.

▲ This image contains 1 million different colors. The human eye can distinguish about 10 million different colors.

Vocabulary

A. Answer the questions in complete sentences. The first one has been done for you.

1. The hawk grabbed a mouse with its talons. Did it use its mouth or its feet?

   It used its feet.

2. My computer is unique. Is it different or the same?

   ____

3. My dad's vision is getting worse. Is it hard for him to hear or to see?

   ____

4. He is trying to identify the woman. Does he want to know who she is or stop her?

   ____

5. Porpoises are marine animals. Do they live in the water or in the sky?

   ____

6. Mammals are warm-blooded animals with hair. Are iguanas or kangaroos mammals?

   ____

B. Fill in the blanks using the expressions from the box.

bounce off of	for one thing	made up of

1. You are not kind. ________________, you broke my pencil and never apologized.
2. I like to watch bugs ________________ a light-bulb when I am bored.
3. My class is ________________ five boys and seven girls.

Reading Comprehension

A. Main Ideas. Circle the answer that best completes each statement.

1. Color is made ________.

a. in our brains **b.** when light bounces off of our eyes

2. Seeing colors helps animals to ________.

a. find food **b.** see farther

3. Birds can detect ultraviolet light because ________.

a. they have special eyes **b.** their brains have a special ability

B. Details. Write True or False or Not Given after each statement.

1. Light is changed by the things that it bounces off of. ________

2. Some sea animals can only see ultraviolet light. ________

3. Dogs see fewer colors than people. ________

4. Some birds use ultraviolet light to hunt. ________

5. Mouse trails give off ultraviolet light. ________

6. Some birds only see two main types of color. ________

C. Inferences. Decide which of the statements can be inferred from the passage. Check the correct answers. (Choose two.)

______ **1.** Without color, we would have a hard time telling things apart.

______ **2.** A dog's brain can see only two unique colors.

______ **3.** Most fish can probably see three main types of color.

______ **4.** Light bounces off of a pumpkin and a cherry in different ways.

Writing

A. Organize. Look at the outline of the main ideas in the passage. Use the list of details to fill in the blanks.

- Dogs see two main types of color.
- Birds can see ultraviolet light.
- Our brains see differences in light as color.
- People see three main types of colors.
- Light bounces off of different things in different ways.

OUTLINE	
Main Ideas	**Details**
1. Color is made by our brains.	a. ________________ ________________ b. ________________
2. Different animals see colors differently.	a. ________________ b. ________________ c. ________________

B. Synthesize. Using Organize above, complete the explanation by filling the blanks with the correct words.

How Do We See Light?

1. Light ________ off an object.
2. The ________ enters your eyes.
3. Your eye sends information to your ________.
4. Your brain sees differences in light as ________.

05 UNIT

The Tree of Life

Baobab trees in Tanzania

Guesswork

Discuss your answers to these questions with your classmates.

1. What can you see in the picture?
2. What is that space used for?
3. Can you tell where the space is located?

▲ Morondava, Madagascar: The African Baobab tree is also known as the "upside-down" tree and it's easy to see why. In winter, when the leaves are gone, the bare branches look like roots reaching into the sky.

RH2-05
MP3

▲ Baobab fruit

The Tree of Life

Trees have many uses. They fuel our fires, provide wood for our homes, and give us all sorts of delicious foods. No tree is quite as useful as the baobab, though. In fact, it is so important that natives know it as the "tree of life."

The name makes sense when you consider the things that humans need to survive. The necessities of life are food, water, and shelter. The baobab provides all three and more. Its fruit is highly nutritious and delicious. It can be eaten raw, or it can be made into drinks, soups or

▲ People have used the insides of Baobabs for all sorts of things. They have been homes, bars and toilets.

porridges. Baobabs can store up to 32,000 gallons of water in their massive trunks. During droughts, natives use hollow grass to suck water directly out of the tree. The insides of old baobabs are often hollow. Natives use these spaces to store grain and livestock. Some trunks are so huge that they can house an entire family!

▲ **The Baobab Prison Tree** A very large, hollow baobab south of Derby, Western Australia was used in the 1890s as a prison. This Baobab tree has an opening on one side that leads into it hollowed out interior. It has enough room to hold five prisoners.

Besides the necessities, the Baobab has all sorts of other uses. Its leaves are full of vitamins and can be eaten to protect against illness. The bark can be eaten to protect against malaria, a common and deadly disease. The bark also provides fibers that can be used to make cloth, rope, nets, hats and musical instrument strings. It even regenerates after humans strip it away.

Do you want a Baobab house? You'll have to wait. They take thousands of years to grow that big.

Vocabulary

A. Answer the questions in complete sentences. The first one has been done for you.

1. Water is a necessity of life. Is it needed or not needed?

It is needed.

2. Horses are useful for traveling. Are they thoughtful or helpful?

____

3. Mom said I should consider getting a job. Should I think about it or forget about it?

____

4. I eat raw eggs because they are healthy. Are they cooked or uncooked?

____

5. Tofu is a very nutritious food. Is it healthy or unhealthy?

____

6. The farmers were suffering from a long drought. Were they lacking food or water?

____

B. Complete the sentences by choosing the correct answer.

1. Bob died two years ago. It doesn't make sense that ________.

a. you saw him in the store　　b. everyone was sad

2. I use a bug net to protect against ________.

a. mosquitoes　　b. dirty air

3. We need to paint our house. First we should strip away ________.

a. all the new paint　　b. all the old paint

Reading Comprehension

A. Main Ideas. Circle the answer that best completes each statement.

1. The Baobab is nicknamed the "tree of life" because __________ .

a. it helps people survive
b. it's used to make new life

2. The Baobab is useful in droughts because __________ .

a. it provides a place to store grain
b. it stores massive amounts of water

3. The Baobab's bark __________ .

a. has many uses
b. is highly nutritious

B. Details. Circle the answers that best complete each statement.

1. The baobab's fruit is (1) __________ and can be (2) __________ .

(1) a. huge b. nutritious c. hollow

(2) a. used to store grain b. used to store water c. made into porridge

2. The bark of the baobab (1) __________ and (2) __________ after people take it away.

(1) a. contains vitamins b. is delicious c. protects against malaria

(2) a. grows back b. stores water c. is eaten raw

C. Inferences. Decide which of the statements can be inferred from the passage. Check the correct answers. (Choose two.)

_______ **1.** Baobabs can be very important in places with little water.

_______ **2.** The fruit of the baobab can be stored for a long time.

_______ **3.** Wild animals sometimes make their homes inside baobab trees.

_______ **4.** Old baobabs are often cut down and used for fire wood.

Writing

A. Organize. Place each detail in the correct box.

- protect against illness
- protects against malaria
- stores up to 32,000 gallons of water
- highly nutritious
- hollow space used to store grain and livestock
- used to make cloth, rope, nets, and hats

The Many Uses of the Baobab Tree	
Part of the Baobab	**Use**
Leaves	**a.** provide vitamins **b.** ______________
Trunk	**a.** ______________ **b.** ______________
Bark	**a.** ______________ **b.** ______________
Fruit	**a.** ______________ **b.** can be made into drinks, soups, and porridge

B. Synthesize. Use the chart in Organize above. Complete the conversation between a researcher and a reporter.

Reporter: You tried to show how useful a baobab tree is, by living in one for 3 months?

Researcher: Yes. And not only that, all of my food and water came from it as well. I drank water from its **t**__________ and I ate its highly **n**__________ fruit.

Reporter: That's amazing. Did the baobab have any other **u**__________?

Researcher: Well, I also made clothes out of its **b**__________!

06 UNIT

Not So Innocent

1

The Great Banyan, located in the Indian Botanical Gardens in India

2

A banyan tree growing around another tree

Guesswork

Discuss your answers to these questions with your classmates.

1. Describe the trees in the pictures. How are they special?
2. Look at picture 2. What is happening?
3. How many trees do you see in picture 1?

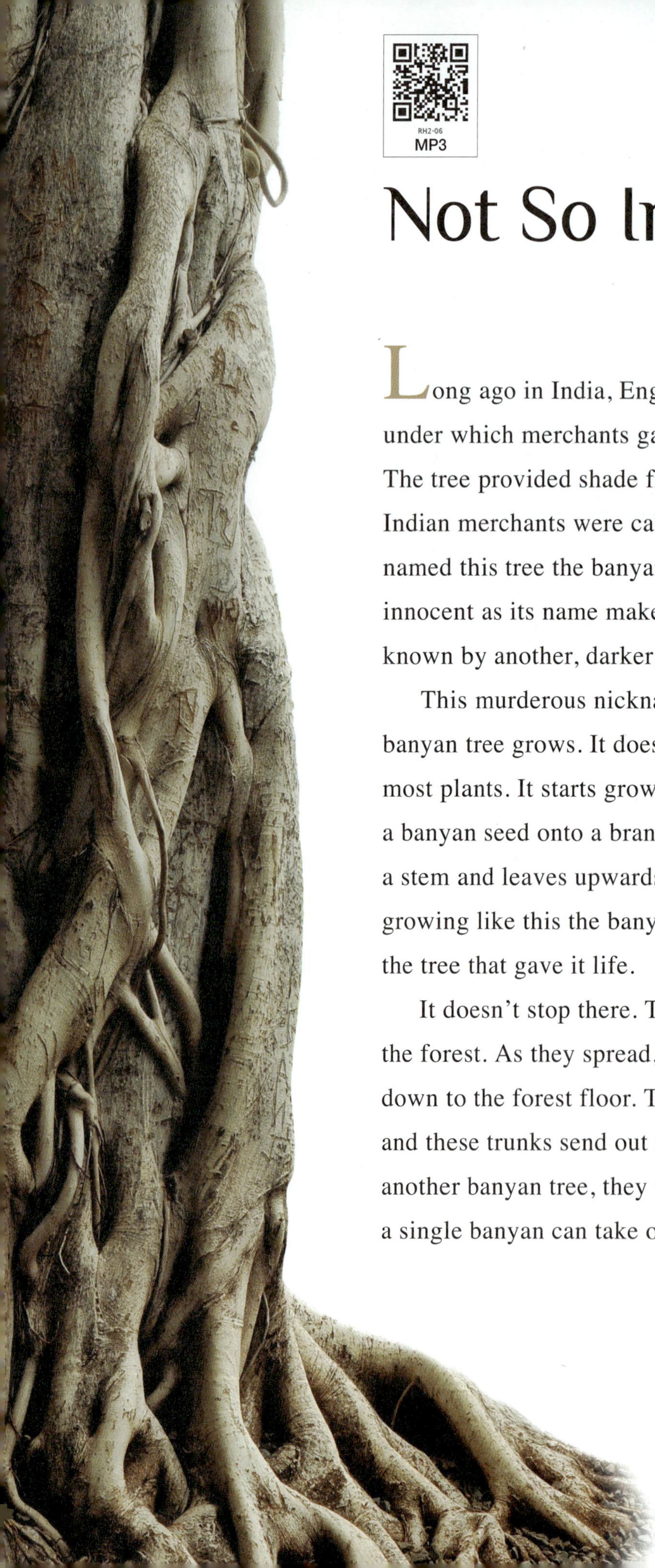

RH2-06
MP3

Not So Innocent

Long ago in India, English travelers noticed a huge tree under which merchants gathered to sell their merchandise. The tree provided shade from the hot Indian sun. As the Indian merchants were called "banya," the travelers named this tree the banyan tree. The banyan isn't as innocent as its name makes it sound, though. It is also known by another, darker, name: "strangler fig."

This murderous nickname describes exactly how the banyan tree grows. It doesn't start life in the ground, like most plants. It starts growing on other trees. A bird drops a banyan seed onto a branch, and the seed sprouts. It sends a stem and leaves upwards, and roots downwards. By growing like this the banyan tree eventually "strangles" the tree that gave it life.

It doesn't stop there. The branches spread out through the forest. As they spread, the banyan tree sends roots down to the forest floor. These roots become new trunks, and these trunks send out new branches. If it meets another banyan tree, they will merge together. In this way, a single banyan can take over an entire forest.

▲ The banyan doesn't just grow on other trees. It can grow on roofs, walls, or even on itself. (From left: Ta Prohm temple, Cambodia; trees growing on a stone wall, Hong Kong)

The Great Banyan, in the Indian Botanical Gardens, was the widest tree in the world until 1925. The original trunk had to be removed due to disease. What is left of it covers 14,500 square meters. That's more than two soccer fields put together!

▲ **Banyan tree with Hindu temples** -Thomas Daniell, 1796; In Hindu culture, the banyan is considered sacred. It is said to be the current resting place of the god Krishna.

Vocabulary

A. Circle the correct answer and write it in the blank.

		a.	b.
1.	When people gather they are ________ .	**a.** together	**b.** apart
2.	Merchandise can be found at a ________ .	**a.** store	**b.** park
3.	To be murderous is to ________ .	**a.** live	**b.** kill
4.	A seed needs ________ to sprout.	**a.** water	**b.** pressure
5.	To remove something is to ________ it away.	**a.** take	**b.** put
6.	The trunk of a tree helps it to ________ .	**a.** breath	**b.** stand
7.	The branch of a tree holds the ________ .	**a.** leaves	**b.** roots
8.	To strangle someone is to ________ them.	**a.** push	**b.** squeeze
9.	A merchant is someone who ________ goods.	**a.** makes	**b.** sells
10.	An innocent person is not ________ .	**a.** good	**b.** guilty

B. Draw lines to make correct sentences. Write the completed sentences below.

1.	My mother •	• take over •	• your entire house if you aren't careful.
2.	Caterpillars •	• sends out •	• without wings, but change into butterflies.
3.	Cockroaches can •	• start life •	• the mail around 8 o'clock every morning.

(1) My mother ______________________________

(2) Caterpillars ______________________________

(3) Cockroaches can ______________________________

Reading Comprehension

A. Main Ideas. Complete the statement by circling the correct choice for each blank.

The passage is mainly about the **1.** _________ of **2.** _________. So the main idea is that **3.** _________.

1. a. growth   b. name

2. a. a unique tree   b. a special garden

3. a. the Indian Botanical Gardens house the widest tree in the world
b. one banyan tree can spread through an entire forest

B. Details. Complete each sentence with the correct answer.

1. The banyan tree got its name from _________.
a. the way that it grows
b. the people that used it

2. When the banyan tree sends roots down to ground, they become _________.
a. branches
b. trunks

3. The Great Banyan is no longer the widest tree in the world because _________.
a. its original trunk was removed
b. it covers only 14,500 meters

C. Inferences. Read each statement and decide if you think it is likely or unlikely. Check the appropriate box.

		Likely	Unlikely
1.	Banyan trees sometimes strangle people.	☐	☐
2.	A single banyan tree can appear to be many different trees.	☐	☐
3.	Indian merchants liked the banyan tree because it killed other trees.	☐	☐
4.	Banyan trees could be a danger to tree farms.	☐	☐

Writing

A. Organize. Write each statement in the correct box.

- It is also known as the "strangler fig."
- It sends roots down from the branches of other trees.
- One banyan tree can spread through an entire forest.
- It provided shade for merchants called "banya."

EVENT or topic
"The banyan tree"

HOW did it get its name?
____
____
____

HOW does it grow?
____
____
____

WHY is it special?
____
____
____

WHAT is its other nickname?
____
____

B. Synthesize. Using Organize above, fill in the details in the "Wanted" poster below.

WANTED!

The __________ Tree
Also Known As: The __________ Fig
This murderous tree has __________ through countless forests.
It sends its __________ down from __________, and strangles other trees.
If you have information about this tree's whereabouts please call: 603-617-4025

07 UNIT

Just for Fun

Guesswork

Discuss your answers to these questions with your classmates.

1. What are these people doing? Does it seem dangerous?
2. Why do you think the people are doing this?
3. Does this seem like fun to you?

▲ Extreme Ironing on Rivelin Needle, Sheffield, UK

Just for Fun

RH2-07
MP3

People love games. And more than just playing them, we love to win. Competition is often fierce. Just take a look at the fans and players of the World Cup! But not all competitions are that serious. Some are just for fun.

▲ Every Wife Carrying race includes a water obstacle.

Wife Carrying

In this *Finnish sport, which started as a joke, competitors carry their wives through an obstacle course. There are several different methods of carrying. Some put their wives over their shoulders. Others carry them in front. But most racers have their wives hang upside down off of their backs. It's not an easy race, but it is fun! And the winner of the race is usually awarded his wife's weight in beer!

▲ During Cheese-Rolling, an ambulance waits at the bottom of Cooper's Hill. At least one person gets injured every year.

Cheese-Rolling

The annual cheese-rolling competition is held at Cooper's Hill, near Gloucester, England. It's fast, funny, and often painful! A big wheel of hard cheese is rolled down the hill and the contestants chase after it. The hill is so steep that nobody ever stays on their feet, and the racers end up tumbling down the hill just like the cheese!

Extreme Ironing

Ironing is simple, right? So how can it be a sport? Well, why don't you try ironing underwater? Since the sport started in 1999, participants have ironed under the ice of a frozen lake, in a canoe, while skiing, while snowboarding, while parachuting, in the middle of the street, and on top of large statues. What extreme place would you try ironing?

▲ Two men are on their way up Snowdon-1,038 m (3,406 ft) Ranked 4th in British Isles. Extreme ironing has taken place all over the world.

*__Finnish__ of or relating to Finland

Vocabulary

A. Circle the correct answer and write it in the blank.

1. A fierce animal is usually ________. **a.** calm **b.** violent

2. Fans go to a stadium to ________ sports. **a.** play **b.** watch

3. An obstacle is ________ to go around. **a.** difficult **b.** easy

4. To be awarded something is to ________ it. **a.** get **b.** give

5. An annual celebration happens every ________. **a.** month **b.** year

6. A painful fall ________. **a.** scares **b.** hurts

7. To chase something is to ________ it. **a.** bring **b.** follow

8. To be frozen is to be a ________. **a.** solid **b.** liquid

9. A statue is a piece of ________. **a.** furniture **b.** art

10. A canoe is used to travel across ________. **a.** deserts **b.** lakes

B. Draw lines to make correct sentences. Write the completed sentences below.

1. Bats •	• go down the hill on your bike •	• and sleep all day.
2. Don't •	• hang upside down in a cave •	• or you will get hurt.
3. I can't •	• stay on my feet when I am on boats •	• because they make me feel sick.

(1) Bats ________________________________

(2) Don't ________________________________

(3) I can't ________________________________

Reading Comprehension

A. Main Ideas. Circle the correct answer to the question.

1. What is the main idea of this passage?

a. Fierce competitions aren't usually very much fun.
b. Some competitions are more fun than others.
c. Some competitions are held only for fun.
d. The most fun competitions are the strangest.

B. Details. Write True or False or Not Given after each statement.

1. In wife-carrying, some racers carry their wives in front. ________

2. In the cheese-rolling competition, the winner eats the cheese. ________

3. The cheese-rolling competition is held near Glouchester, England. ________

4. Extreme ironing has been done over water and underwater. ________

5. The winner of extreme ironing is awarded beer. ________

6. Extreme ironing happens once a year. ________

C. Inferences. Decide which of the statements can be inferred from the passage. Check the correct answers. (Choose two.)

______ **1.** Extreme ironing is popular among housewives.

______ **2.** In the cheese-rolling competition, competitors enjoy tumbling down the hill.

______ **3.** In wife-carrying, the wives usually drink the winner's beer.

______ **4.** In extreme ironing, the clothes aren't always ironed very well.

Writing

A. Organize. Place each detail in the correct box.

- held once a year
- started in 1999
- contestants tumble down a hill
- winner awarded wife's weight in beer
- has been done in the middle of the street

Competition	Details
Wife Carrying	**a.** ______________________ **b.** started as a joke
Cheese Rolling	**a.** ______________________ **b.** ______________________
Extreme Ironing	**a.** ______________________ **b.** ______________________

B. Synthesize. Use the chart in Organize above. Complete the conversation between a reporter and a fan of strange competitions.

Reporter: What strange __________ have you attended?

Fan: I've seen wife-__________, cheese-__________, and __________ ironing.

Reporter: Which was your favorite?

Fan: I loved cheese-__________. Watching the contestants __________ down that hill was so funny.

Reporter: What else did you find entertaining?

Fan: Wife-__________ was fun too. Even though it started as a __________, many racers took it seriously.

08 UNIT
Fame and Fortune

Guesswork

Discuss your answers to these questions with your classmates.

1. What is the woman doing?

2. Is she famous? Does she want to be famous?

3. How could she become a professional singer?

▲ In the tenth season of the American Idol series, Steven Tyler and Jennifer Lopez joined Randy Jackson as judges.

▲ Kelly Clarkson, the first winner of American Idol, is performing a concert.

RH2-08
MP3

Fame and Fortune

Do you like to sing? Do you want to be famous? Then just try out for an idol show! Anybody can audition. It doesn't even matter if you are a good singer or not. Of course, bad singing won't win you the competition, but if you sing badly enough you might still become famous!

For contestants, idol competitions offer fame and fortune. Most contestants are just normal people. They might practice singing in the shower, or in front of friends. Idol shows aim to discover their hidden talents. Winning a competition often completely changes a winner's life. They record albums, perform concerts, and make lots of money.

▲ In 2009, over 9000 people came to Amway Arena in Orlando, Florida to audition for American Idol.

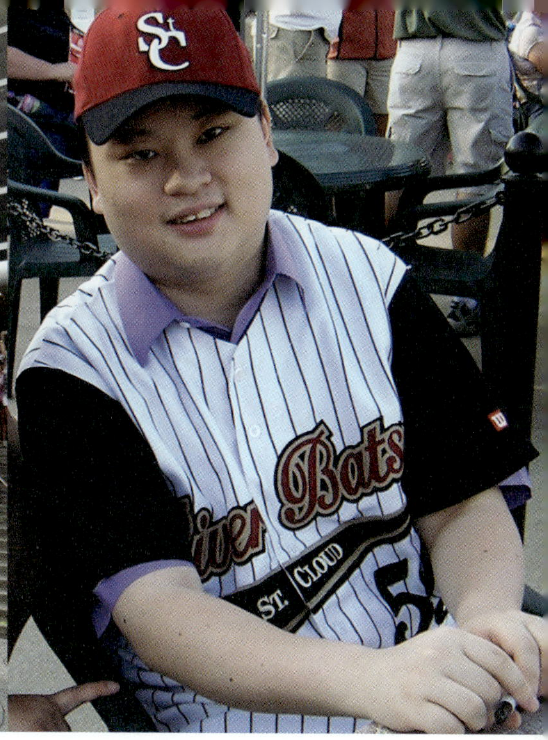

▲ William Hung has released 3 albums, been on numerous television shows, made movies, and even has a documentary about his life, all thanks to his terrible singing!

For television viewers, idol is also great fun. The audience gets to watch amazing performances by talented contestants. Some performances are the same high quality as professional pop concerts. Even the bad singers are great entertainment. Their mistakes and off-key singing are often hilarious. Some are so bad that they become famous! William Hung, one especially terrible singer, even signed a record deal. People bought his CDs just because his singing was so funny!

Now, new kinds of talent competitions are becoming popular. They feature magicians, dancers, jugglers, sword-eaters and all sorts of other entertainers. Like idol, these shows have their fair share of embarrassing mistakes and ridiculous performances. And like idol, they offer huge prizes: sometimes as much as $1,000,000! So what talent will you share with the world?

Did You Know?

The first idol show appeared in Britain in 2001. Now idol shows appear in almost every country in the world, and are worth over $8 billion.

Vocabulary

A. Circle the answer that fits best with the word in red.

1. audition	know / try / hear
2. fortune	strength / wealth / fear
3. hidden	search / skip / hang
4. completely	all / some / almost
5. perform	show / listen / watch
6. talent	skill / idea / action
7. professional	joking / serious / mistaken
8. hilarious	famous / fantastic / funny
9. ridiculous	sizable / silly / soft
10. share	seize / hold / give

B. Complete the sentences by choosing the correct answer.

1. My brother is going to be famous! He just signed a deal with ________.

a. a record company
b. a bear
c. our mother
d. a supermarket

2. Your music sounds the same as ________. Did you copy me?

a. yours
b. his
c. mine
d. Brian's

3. I'm going to try out for ________.

a. the baseball team
b. English class
c. cooking
d. a job at the supermarket

Reading Comprehension

A. Main Ideas. Complete the statement by circling the correct choice for each blank.

The passage is mainly about the **1.** __________ of **2.** __________ . So the main idea is that **3.** __________ .

1. a. entertainment b. talents

2. a. winners b. idol shows

3. a. idol shows are great fun for entertainers and audiences alike
b. winners of idol shows make lots of money and become famous

B. Details. Complete each sentence by circling the correct choice.

1. Audiences like idol shows because they __________ .

a. provide great entertainment
b. explain how to sing like real pop stars
c. offer a chance to become rich and famous

2. Some idol performers become famous even though __________ .

a. they can't sing very well
b. they are already rich and famous
c. their performances are the same high quality as professional pop stars'

C. Inferences. Read each statement and decide if you think it is likely or unlikely. Check the appropriate box.

	Likely	Unlikely
1. Many famous pop stars try out for Idol shows.	☐	☐
2. Bad singers sometimes win idol shows.	☐	☐
3. Some people try out for idol shows because they want to become rich.	☐	☐
4. Many normal people dream about being pop stars.	☐	☐

Writing

A. Organize. Place each detail in the correct box.

- could win an idol show and become famous
- enjoy watching contestants perform
- sometimes perform as well as professional pop stars
- could become famous because they are funny

	Idol Shows
good singers	a. ____________________ b. ____________________
bad singers	a. ____________________
audiences	a. ____________________

B. Synthesize. Using Organize above, fill in the missing information in the advertisement for idol show auditions.

Idol Show A__________!

September 20th at the Verizon Wireless Arena

Do you sing in the shower? Do you sing for your friends?

Do you want to be f__________?

Come t__________ out!

Anyone can audition, and anyone could w__________ and become a famous p__________ s__________!

Even bad singers can become f__________ if they are f__________ enough!

Don't want to try out? Then just come and watch the c__________ perform!

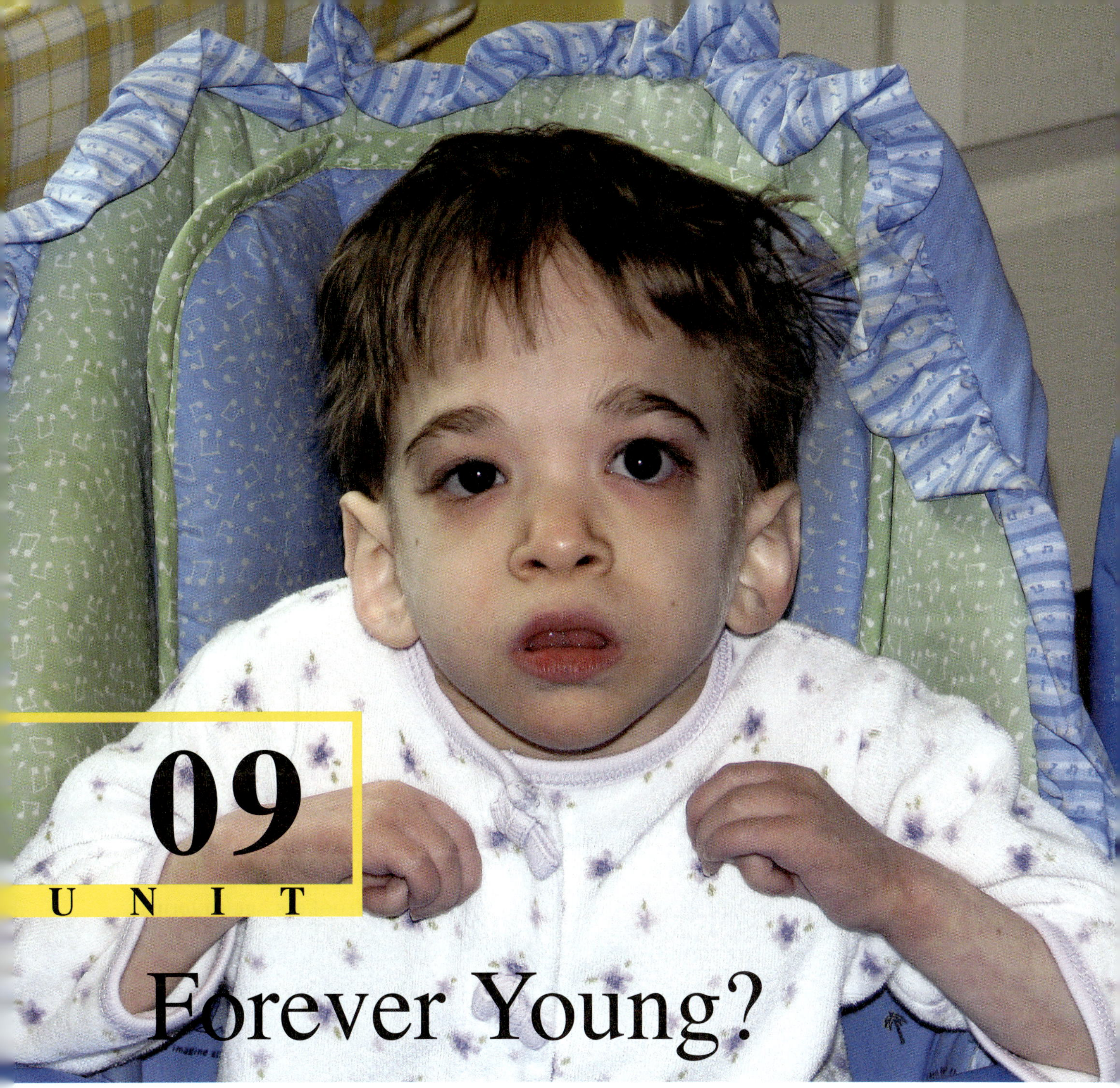

UNIT 09
Forever Young?

Guesswork

Discuss your answers to these questions with your classmates.

1. What do you think of the girl in the picture?
2. Does she seem strange at all? How do you think she is different?
3. How old do you think the girl is?

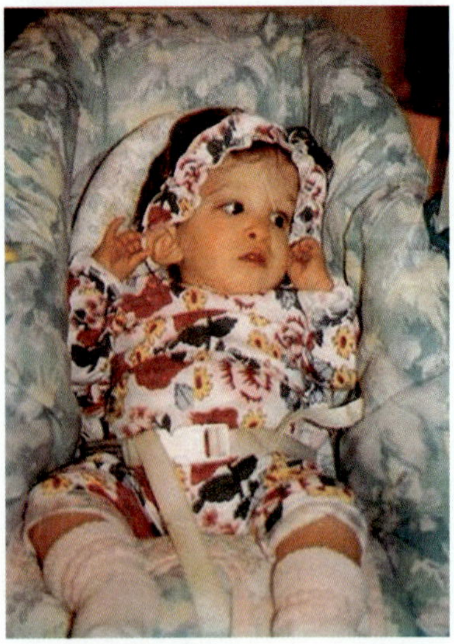
▲ Brooke at 3 years old

RH2-09
MP3

Forever Young?

Brooke Greenberg is 17 years old. Like most teenagers she loves to go shopping with her mother. She is not like most teenagers, though. She can't ride a bike, or play sports. In fact, she can't even speak. Brooke's body is still that of an infant.

Brooke does not age in the same way that other people do. Her hair and nails are the only parts of her body that grow normally. All of her other parts age at different rates, but they don't grow. Doctors say that her bones are about 10 years old, her teeth are 8 years old, and her mind is similar to that of a one year-old.

When people see Brooke, they ask how old she is. Brooke's mother doesn't try to explain because it would be too complicated. She tells them Brooke's age in terms of months, not years. It's easier for her to just say, "Brooke is 16 months old."

Scientists are trying to discover what makes Brooke so different, but they aren't having much luck. Her condition is unique. There are other kinds of aging diseases, but none quite like hers. There is hope that Brooke will help us better understand how people age. Some even think Brooke might be the key to immortality.

Brooke's mother would be happy if her daughter could help people live better. She doesn't worry too much about that, though. She is happy just to have Brooke as a part of her family.

▲ Brooke, 8, with her younger sister Carly, 5

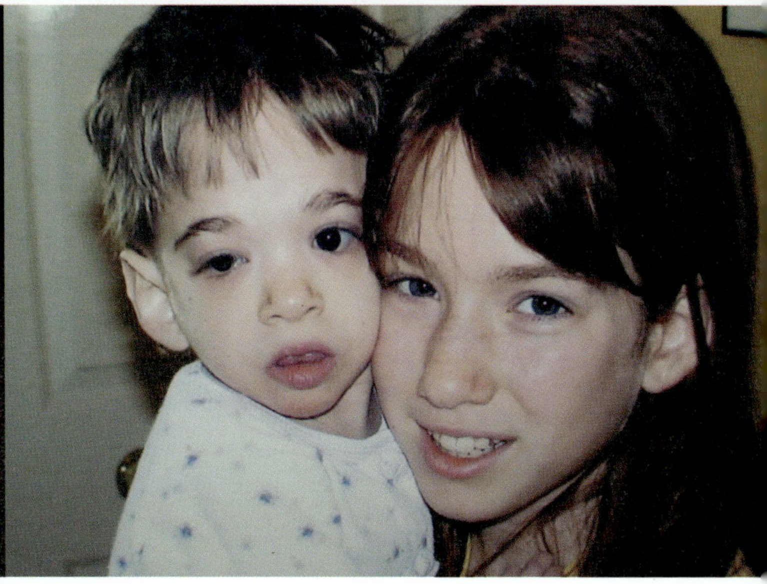

▲ Brooke, 12, and Carly, 9

▲ Brooke, 16, and Carly 13

▲ Brooke at 17 years old

Vocabulary

A. Answer the questions in complete sentences. The first one has been done for you.

1. My sister is an infant. Was she born recently or a long time ago?

She was born recently.

2. Paul can't walk normally. Does he walk strangely or typically?

____

3. Debra is a unique person. Is she typical or different?

____

4. Vampires are thought to be immortal. Do they live forever, or for a short time?

____

5. Without bones, people would feel like jelly. Do bones help us breathe or hold us up?

____

6. My cat never seems to age. Does it seem to stay the same or to always change?

____

B. Draw lines to make complete sentences. Write the completed sentences below.

1.	I don't think of my day •	• many teachers, •	• as a part of this team.
2.	I have had •	• in terms of hours– •	• I think in terms of minutes.
3.	I promise that •	• I will work hard •	• but none quite like you.

(1) I don't think of my day ______________________________

(2) I have had ______________________________

(3) I promise that ______________________________

Reading Comprehension

A. Main Ideas. Circle the answer that best completes the statement.

1. Brooke is different from most teenagers because ________.

a. she likes to go shopping
b. she ages at a strange rate
c. her hair and nails grow fast
d. she is younger than most teenagers

B. Details. Write True or False or Not Given after each statement.

1. Brooke's bones age normally. ________

2. Brooke's mother thinks that she is really 16 months old. ________

3. Brooke's body parts all age at different rates. ________

4. Scientists believe they can cure her. ________

5. Brooke may teach us about the aging process. ________

6. Brooke's mother thinks she will live forever. ________

C. Inferences. Decide which of the statements can be inferred from the passage. Check the correct answers. (Choose one.)

______ **1.** Brooke's heart is about the same age as her bones.

______ **2.** Scientists are curious about Brooke's condition.

______ **3.** People see Brooke and realize that she is 16 years old.

______ **4.** Brooke's mother wants her to be the key to immortality.

Writing

A. Organize. Use the options below to complete the chart about Brooke Greenberg.

- Brooke's mind
- how people age
- Brooke's bones
- Brooke's hair and nails
- Brooke's teeth
- the key to immortality

1. Brooke is like most teenagers.

a. Brooke loves to go shopping with her mother.
b. ______________________ grow normally.

2. Brooke is a unique teenager.

a. Brooke's body is still that of an infant.
b. ______________________ are about 10 years old.
c. ______________________ are 8 years old.
d. ______________________ is similar to that of a one year-old.

3. Brooke could help the world.

a. Brooke might be ______________________
b. Brooke will help us better understand ______________________

B. Synthesize. Using Organize above, complete the blanks in the advertisement for a documentary on the life of Brooke Greenberg.

A Teenage Baby

Brooke Greenberg is the age of a __________, but
her body is still that of an __________!
Her condition is __________.
Scientists hope she will teach us more about __________ __________ __________.
Her mother is just happy to have her as part of the family.

10 UNIT

A Daring Esca

Guesswork

Discuss your answers to these questions with your classmates.

1. What are the people in the picture doing?
2. Does it look scary? Would you ever do it?
3. Can skydiving be useful, or is it just a fun activity?

D. B. Cooper hijacked a Boeing 727, Northwest Orient Flight in the United States on November 24, 1971, received $200,000 in ransom, and then escaped by parachuting from the plane.

A Daring Escape

RH2-10
MP3

▲ Larry Carr (right), the FBI agent overseeing the case, now believes the hijacker may have taken his name from a French comic book. The Dan Cooper comic book was popular in France in the 1960s and early 1970s. One issue published around the time of the hijacking shows the character parachuting.

Most everything about D.B. Cooper is a mystery, even his real name. If he is still alive, he probably prefers it this way. After all, he is responsible for the world's only unsolved airplane hijacking.

In 1971, on a flight heading over Portland Oregon, a man calling himself Dan Cooper handed a note to a flight attendant. It read: "I have a bomb. You are being hijacked. Do what I say." The woman was scared, but she did exactly what he told her to do, as she did not want the passengers to panic.

Cooper demanded that the plane land, and requested four parachutes and $200,000. After he got what he wanted, Cooper allowed the passengers to leave the plane. He then ordered the pilot to take off again, even though there was a thunderstorm approaching. Once they were up in the air, Cooper told the crew to move to the front of the plane. While they were up front, the crew heard a loud noise from the back. They rushed back, and discovered the door open and cold rain blowing into the plane.

There was no sign of Cooper, and the money and two parachutes were missing. He must have jumped into the storm! The FBI searched the ground below for days, but never found Cooper. To this day no one knows who he was, why he did it, or even if he survived his daring escape.

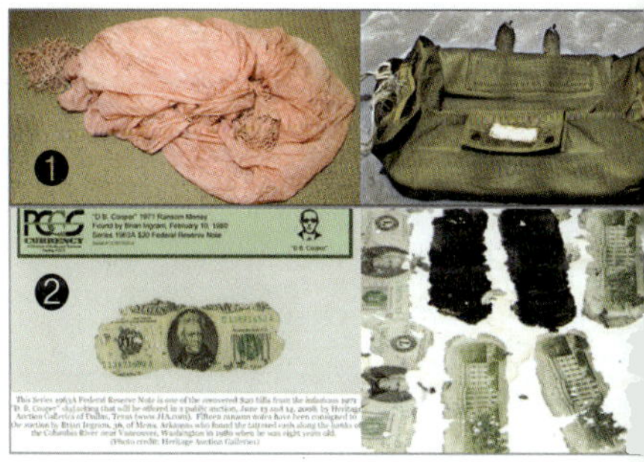

▲ ① One of the parachutes left behind by Cooper and the canvas bag it came in. Cooper asked for four chutes in all; he jumped with two. ② Some of the stolen $20 bills were found by a young boy in 1980.

Vocabulary

A. Answer the questions in complete sentences. The first one has been done for you.

1. Grace prefers pizza over chicken. Does she like to eat pizza or chicken better?

   She likes to eat pizza better.

2. Michelle handed the man a newspaper. Did she give it to him or take it from him?

   ____

3. My teacher demanded that I sit down. Did he watch me sit down or tell me to sit down?

   ____

4. When his mother appeared, the boy panicked. Was the boy scared or angry?

   ____

5. Ryan requested that I call him back. Did he ask politely or rudely?

   ____

6. The athletes rushed onto the field. Did they move slowly or quickly?

   ____

B. Fill in the blanks using the expressions from the box.

responsible for	after all	take off

1. I should be the first to try this machine. ______________, I'm the person who invented it.
2. You are ______________ the broken window. You should pay for it.
3. We will ______________ shortly, so everyone should now fasten their seatbelts.

Reading Comprehension

A. Main Ideas. Complete the statement by circling the correct choice for each blank.

The passage is mainly about the **1.** _________ of **2.** _________ . So the main idea is that **3.** _________ .

1. a. identity b. mystery

2. a. a famous criminal b. an expensive airplane

3. a. how D.B. Cooper hijacked an airplane and then escaped
b. why D.B Cooper decided to ask for $200,000 and four parachutes

B. Details. Complete each sentence by circling the correct choice.

1. The flight attendant followed Cooper's directions because _________ .

a. she didn't want the plane to crash
b. she didn't want to frighten anyone
c. she wanted Cooper to get $200,000

2. The crew moved to the front of the plane _________ .

a. because it was safer there
b. so that Cooper couldn't see them
c. after Cooper ordered them to move there

C. Inferences. Decide which of the statements can be inferred from the passage. Check the correct answers. (Choose two.)

_______ **1.** Before hijacking the plane, Cooper already knew he would escape by jumping.

_______ **2.** The FBI gave Cooper a broken parachute.

_______ **3.** The FBI doesn't know Cooper's real name.

_______ **4.** Cooper was lying when he said that he had a bomb.

Writing

A. Organize. Arrange the events of Dan Cooper's hijacking in the correct order.

1	A man hands a note to a flight attendant on a flight heading over Portland, Oregon.
	The plane takes off again.
	The man is brought four parachutes and $200,000.
	The man jumps out of the back of the plane with the money.
	The man demands that the plane land.
	The passengers get off the plane.

B. Synthesize. Fill in the blanks of the Wanted Poster for Dan Cooper.

WANTED: $500,000 Reward

A man calling himself Dan Cooper hijacked a plane
__________ __________ Portland, Oregon.
He demanded that it land, and was brought
__________ and __________.
He then allowed the passengers to __________ __________ the plane and demanded that the plane __________ __________ again.
While the plane was in the air, Cooper __________ __________ with the $200,000.
To the right, is a police sketch of what Cooper looked like then, and what he may look like now.
Please call the FBI at 603-617-4025 if you have information about this crime.

UNIT 11

Sweet Disaster

Guesswork

Discuss your answers to these questions with your classmates.

1. What do you think the picture shows?
2. Do you think people were injured?
3. What do you think caused all this damage?

View of the North End, Boston neighborhood (2006)

Panorama of the Molasses Disaster site in the North End (1919)

▲ It took 87,000 hours to clean all the molasses off the streets, businesses, homes, and cars. Boston Harbor was brown with molasses until summer.

RH2-11
MP3

▲ **Blackstrap molasses**
Molasses is a sugary liquid used to sweeten food and drinks.

Sweet Disaster

In 1919, there was a sudden flood in Boston, Massachusetts. 21 people were killed and 150 were injured. The flood wasn't caused by a storm, or even by a broken dam. And it didn't come from a river or a lake. In fact, the flood wasn't even made of water. It was a flood of molasses.

A tank of molasses 50 feet tall and 90 feet wide used to stand in downtown Boston. It's gone now. One morning in January, something went wrong and it burst open. 2.3 million gallons of molasses rushed into the streets of Boston. The heavy liquid formed a wave between 8 and 15 feet high. It moved at a speed of 35 miles per hour. It

▲ Some people, farther away from the flood, were knocked to the ground by a blast of warm sweet air. A truck was picked up and thrown into Boston Harbor.

▲ The explosion turned this elevated train structure into a twisted mass of metal.

was so powerful that it knocked over buildings and even lifted a train off of its tracks. Needless to say, many people and animals were crushed to death. Many others drowned after they were trapped in the waist deep mess.

One boy told his story of surviving the flood. He remembers being picked up by the wave, and then slammed into the ground by the sticky liquid. His throat filled with molasses and he passed out. When he woke up he saw his entire family staring down at him.

The people of Boston were angry about the disaster. Not everyone was lucky like the boy. They sued the molasses company. Eventually they won 6.6 million dollars in damages.

Did You Know?

The molasses company knew that the tank was leaking, but they didn't fix it. Instead they painted it brown, so that nobody could see the molasses leaking out.

Vocabulary

A. Circle the answer that fits best with the word in red.

1. burst break / fall / lift
2. rush smoothly / slowly / quickly
3. wave water / sand / air
4. track road / stairs / river
5. sticky olive oil / water / honey
6. stare listen / look / feel
7. trapped changed / stuck / hurt
8. gone hurt / missing / surprised
9. lift down / over / up
10. waist middle / top / bottom

B. Choose the answer that best completes each sentence.

1. We thought we were going to win, but something went wrong and ________.

   a. we lost b. we won

2. Did you know that the fastest trains can move at a speed of ________?

   a. 431 km/h b. incredibly fast

3. After the accident, Jake passed out and ________.

   a. kept screaming in pain b. woke up 5 minutes later

Reading Comprehension

A. Main Ideas. Circle the correct answer for each question.

1. How was the flood of molasses deadly?

a. It was sweet and messy.
b. It was sticky and heavy.

2. What caused the flood?

a. a great storm
b. a broken tank

B. Details. Write True or False or Not Given after each statement.

1. The tank of molasses was 50 feet tall and 90 feet wide. ________

2. Many molasses company employees were killed by the flood. ________

3. The wave of molasses crushed buildings and drowned people. ________

4. When the boy woke up he was slammed by a wave of molasses. ________

5. The people of Boston won a lot of money from the molasses company. ________

6. The tank held 3.2 million gallons of molasses before it burst. ________

C. Inferences. Decide which of the statements can be inferred from the passage. Check the correct answers. (Choose two.)

______ **1.** Many people expected that the tank of molasses would burst.

______ **2.** People were happy to have a flood of free molasses.

______ **3.** It was the molasses company's fault that the tank burst.

______ **4.** The molasses was difficult to clean up.

Writing

A. Organize. Write each statement in the correct box.

- A flood of molasses burst out of a broken molasses tank.
- It happened in January of 1919.
- They sued the molasses company for 6.6 million.
- Boston Molasses Disaster
- It happened in downtown Boston, Massachusetts.

WHAT happened?

____

____

____

WHEN did it happen?

____

____

____

EVENT or topic

"______________________

______________"

WHERE did it happen?

____

____

____

WHAT did the people do?

____

____

____

B. Synthesize. Use the chart in Organize above. Complete the conversation between a survivor of the molasses flood and a reporter 40 years after the disaster.

Reporter: Tell me about the __________ __________ of January, 1919.

Survivor: Well, a huge tank of molasses __________ __________ and flooded downtown __________.

Reporter: Were many people hurt?

Survivor: Yes, 21 died. The people of Boston __________ the __________ __________ for 6.6 million dollars.

UNIT 12
Gone

Guesswork

Discuss your answers to these questions with your classmates.

1. How does this picture make you feel?

2. Why don't we have more than just the skeletons of dinosaurs?

3. Do you know why the dinosaurs died?

▲ Dinosaurs ruled the earth for quite a long time. Modern humans have only been around for about 60,000 years; dinosaurs existed for over 160 million years.

RH2-12
MP3

Gone

Dinosaurs ruled the earth for over 160 million years. Then suddenly, about 65 million years ago, every dinosaur on Earth died. What happened?

It had to be something terrible, and scientists think they know what it was. In 1978 a geologist found a giant crater in Mexico. It was about 180 km wide. Scientists figured out that it was created by an asteroid. By looking at the rocks, scientists measured the age of the crater. They found that it was made about 65 million years ago—around the same time that dinosaurs went extinct.

The asteroid hit the earth with great force. It released about 2,000,000 times more energy than the world's largest atomic bomb. The heat killed many things immediately and forest fires spread across the world. The impact created a mega-tsunami, a giant ocean wave that was thousands of feet high. It also sent shock waves through the earth, creating earthquakes and volcanic eruptions across the globe.

Amazingly, some dinosaurs survived these disasters. But they didn't survive for long. Dust and ash in the sky blocked the sun's light for years, dramatically cooling down the earth. As the weather cooled, plants started dying. Soon, everything that ate them started dying as well. In a short time dinosaurs were completely gone.

Maybe we're lucky that they are extinct. If dinosaurs were still around there wouldn't be any room for us.

▲ (top) Illustration of the impact of an asteroid a few kilometers across; (bottom) Impact crater in Arizona, USA. Impact craters are formed when a large meteoroid, asteroid or comet smashes into a planet or a satellite.

▲ **A brachiosaurus skeleton at Natural History Museum in Berlin** The largest dinosaur was about twice as large as a blue whale and the smallest was around the size of a pigeon.

Vocabulary

A. Answer the questions in complete sentences. The first one has been done for you.

1. The geologist discovered gold in the mountain. Does he work with rocks or trees?

He works with rocks.

2. There is a giant crater in Mexico. Is it a hill or a hole?

____

3. John measured the couch to see if it would fit. Did he check how comfortable it is or how long it is?

____

4. Atomic bombs are very powerful. Are they used in war or for construction?

____

5. When the bomb hit the ground, I felt the impact in my feet. Did I feel the explosion or the landing?

____

6. Native Americans used ash to draw pictures. Did they use mud or the remains of a burnt stick?

____

B. Fill in the blanks using the expressions from the box.

sent shock waves	any room for	as well

1. We're going to the movies. You can come ______________.

2. The explosion ______________ through our house.

3. I don't think I have ______________ dessert. Let's drink some tea instead.

Reading Comprehension

A. Main Ideas. Circle the correct answer for each question.

1. What caused the extinction of the dinosaurs?

a. a crater **b.** an asteroid
c. a geologist **d.** an atomic bomb

2. Which thing DIDN'T kill dinosaurs after the asteroid struck?

a. fires **b.** earthquakes
c. tornadoes **d.** floods

B. Details. Circle the answers that best complete each statement.

1. The asteroid hit the earth about (1) __________ years ago and made a crater about (2) __________ km wide.

(1) **a.** 65 million **b.** 160 million **c.** 2,000,000

(2) **a.** 1978 **b.** 180 **c.** 160 million

2. Some dinosaurs survived the first (1) __________, but then they were killed when the earth (2) __________.

(1) **a.** explosion **b.** disasters **c.** extinction

(2) **a.** cooled down **b.** hit an asteroid **c.** blocked the sun's light

C. Inferences. Decide which of the statements can be inferred from the passage. Check the correct answers. (Choose two.)

_______ **1.** Some dinosaurs might have survived in the ocean.

_______ **2.** Scientists know how to determine how old rocks are.

_______ **3.** Geologists had been searching for the crater for many years.

_______ **4.** If a large asteroid struck the earth today, it would kill many people and animals.

Writing

A. Organize. Place each detail in the correct box.

- a mega-tsunami
- ash and dust in the sky
- earthquakes and volcanic eruptions
- change in the weather
- forest fires

The Asteroid Impact	
Immediate Effects	Long-term Effects

B. Synthesize. Using Organize above, complete the missing information in this diagram of the asteroid impact.

1. Asteroid hits the earth.
2. The impact sends shock waves through the __________, causing __________ and __________ eruptions.
3. Heat from its impact starts __________ __________.
4. __________ and __________ float in the sky, blocking the __________.

UNIT 13

Zombie Ants!

Guesswork

Discuss your answers to these questions with your classmates.

1. What is wrong with the ant in the picture?
2. Is it alive or dead?
3. What do you think is growing on the ant?

▲ The ant froze dead in its tracks after the fungus overtook its body.

▲ A group of zombies, at the shooting of a zombie movie

RH2-13
MP3

Zombie Ants!

Have you ever seen a zombie movie? Zombies are terrifying. A disease infects a person and kills them, but the victim doesn't stay dead. They wake up again as a zombie! Only now the disease is controlling their dead body, and using it to infect more people.

Zombies aren't just in movies, though. There are zombies in the natural world too. They are made by a special kind of fungus that only infects and kills carpenter ants.

When an ant is infected, the fungus takes control of its brain. The fungus makes it climb up a certain kind of plant and bite onto the bottom of a leaf. The ant dies soon after. But its mouth keeps the dead body attached to the leaf. The fungus starts growing, using the ant's dead body for food.

The fungus makes the zombie ant bite onto leaves that are close to 10 inches above the ground, and on the northwest side of the plant. This is exactly where the fungus grows best. This location also provides a convenient way for the fungus to reproduce. From under the leaf, the fungus drops spores onto the forest floor, infecting ants that are walking below.

Luckily carpenter ants live high in the trees away from the forest floor. Maybe they realize it is the one place where they are safe from becoming zombies!

▲ The fungus that infects the ants has been around for at least 48 million years. This means it is older than the Himalayan Mountains.

▲ Carpenter ant

▲ **A water oak damaged by carpenter ants**
The fungus turns usually carpenter ants into zombies. The ants nest high in the canopy of a forest. When carpenter ants nest, they hollow out a series of tunnels in wood.

Vocabulary

A. Circle the correct answer and write it in the blank.

1. A terrifying event is very ________ . **a.** calming **b.** scary

2. A victim is some who is ________ by something. **a.** healed **b.** hurt

3. A fungus is a kind of ________ . **a.** living thing **b.** chemical

4. To infect someone is to make them ________ . **a.** sick **b.** healthy

5. To attach something is to make it ________ . **a.** break **b.** stick

6. To provide something is to ________ it. **a.** give **b.** take

7. To be convenient is to be ________ . **a.** complicated **b.** easy

8. To reproduce is to make ________ of oneself. **a.** fun **b.** copies

9. To be safe is to not be ________ . **a.** in danger **b.** asleep

10. To realize is to suddenly ________ . **a.** forget **b.** know

B. Read the passage below. Match each phrase in red with its equivalent expression.

Last year, scientists discovered ancient dinosaur bones in a Californian house. The bones were **attached to** the cement walls. The scientists removed the bones, and **soon after** the national museum **took control of** them.

1. stuck to ____________________

2. gained power over ____________________

3. a short time later ____________________

Reading Comprehension

A. Main Ideas. Complete the statement by circling the correct choice for each blank.

The passage is mainly about the **1.** _________ of **2.** _________. So the main idea is that **3.** _________.

1. a. reproduction b. attachment

2. a. a kind of ant b. a kind of fungus

3. a. the fungus infects the ant, controls it, kills it, then grows in its dead body
b. the ant attaches to a leaf and reproduces so that the fungus can control it

B. Details. Write True or False or Not Given after each statement.

1. The fungus kills the ant, and then takes control of it. _________

2. After the ant bites onto the bottom of a leaf, the fungus grows inside it. _________

3. The fungus grows for several days before releasing its spores. _________

4. In zombie movies people die and then wake up as zombies. _________

5. Ants can fight off the fungus after it infects them. _________

6. Ants live far away from where the fungus grows. _________

C. Inferences. Decide which of the statements can be inferred from the passage. Check the correct answers. (Choose two.)

_______ **1.** Zombie movies are based on the way this fungus reproduces.

_______ **2.** The ant knows that it is going to die when it is infected.

_______ **3.** The fungus makes the ant bite onto the leaf because it can grow well there.

_______ **4.** Carpenter ants have strong mouths.

Writing

A. Organize. Write each answer (a-g) in the correct place in the chart.

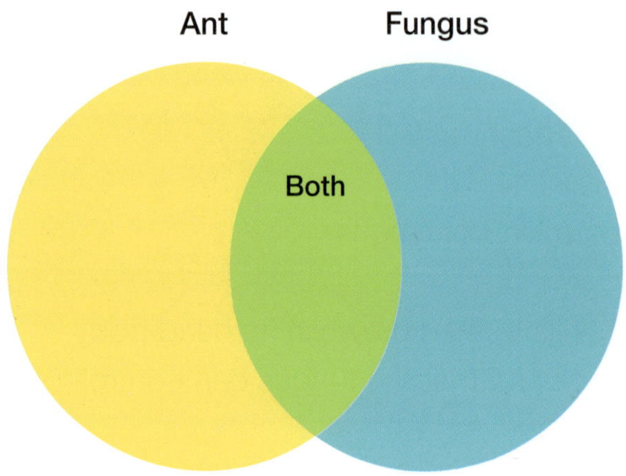

a. dies underneath a leaf
b. takes control of a brain
c. gets infected on the forest floor
d. grows best underneath a leaf
e. lives in the forest
f. lives high in a tree
g. reproduces with spores

B. Synthesize. Using Organize above, fill in the missing information in the reproduction cycle of the fungus.

1. The fungus __________ an ant and takes control of its __________.
2. The fungus makes the __________ climb up a certain kind of plant and __________ onto the bottom of a __________.
3. The fungus __________ the ant and starts growing inside its dead body.
4. The fungus releases __________ onto the ground below. Ants walk over the __________ and become __________.

UNIT 14
Why Stripes?

Guesswork

Discuss your answers to these questions with your classmates.

1. What can you see in the picture?
2. Are the animals difficult to see? Why?
3. Can you think of any other uses for these animals' stripes?

RH2-14
MP3

Why Stripes?

A zebra's stripes aren't just beautiful. They are quite useful in ways that you might never imagine.

Camouflage

A zebra is easy to spot, right? Maybe for us, but not for a lion. Because lions are color-blind, a zebra's stripes are the perfect camouflage. When a zebra is standing still in tall grass, a lion has a hard time spotting it. To the lion, the tall yellow grass and the long black and white stripes all look the same.

A zebra's stripes protect it from a tiny predator too. The tsetse fly might not seem dangerous, but it carries a deadly disease called sleeping sickness. For some reason, it doesn't often bite zebras. Scientists think it gets confused by the zebra's black and white lines.

▲ When zebras are grouped together, their patterning might confuse lions. With all those black and white stripes moving together, a lion may have a hard time picking out an individual zebra.

Identification

We recognize people by their faces. Zebras are different. Because each zebra's stripes are unique, zebras can tell each other apart by their stripes.

▲ **Tsetse fly**
Sleeping sickness is a serious tropical disease which causes great tiredness and often leads to death.

Temperature Control

A zebra's stripes may help it stay a comfortable temperature. Scientists know that their white stripes reflect heat and their black stripes absorb it. This could help them stay cool during the day and warm at night.

Mating

Clear stripes might show that a zebra is healthy. Any injuries would break the striped pattern. A zebra with a broken pattern would look weak, so other zebras would not mate with it.

Vocabulary

A. Circle the answer that fits best with the word in red.

1. stripe — curve / block / line
2. camouflage — show / hide / appear
3. predator — meat / vegetables / sunlight
4. disease — healthy / sick / hungry
5. perfect — new / broken / lost
6. recognize — understand / harm / help
7. unique — slight / extreme / different
8. comfortable — rock / couch / sidewalk
9. absorb — take / give / mark
10. reflect — bounce / break / stick

B. Draw lines to make complete sentences. Write the completed sentences below.

1. Bill should •	• aren't twins •	• telling my sister's cats apart.
2. My uncles •	• pay more attention in class •	• but they look exactly the same.
3. I have •	• a really hard time •	• or he will have a hard time with the test.

(1) Bill should ______________________________

(2) My uncles ______________________________

(3) I have ______________________________

Reading Comprehension

A. Main Ideas. Complete the statement by circling the correct choice for each blank.

The passage is mainly about the **1.** __________ of a zebra's **2.** __________. So the main idea is that **3.** __________.

1. a. camouflage b. uses c. identification

2. a. predators b. temperature c. stripes

3. a. a zebra's predators can identify it by looking at its stripes
b. a zebra's stripes help with temperature control, camouflage, mating, and identification

B. Details. Circle the answers that best complete each statement.

1. The tsetse fly is dangerous because __________.

a. it bites zebras b. it carries disease

2. Zebras can recognize each other by their stripes because __________.

a. the white stripes reflect heat b. each zebra has different stripes

3. A zebra's stripes help with mating because __________.

a. the striped pattern makes injuries easy to see
b. weak zebras have fewer stripes

C. Inferences. Decide which of the statements can be inferred from the passage. Check the correct answers. (Choose two.)

_______ **1.** Scientists know everything about a zebra's stripes.

_______ **2.** Zebras often live alone.

_______ **3.** An injured zebra is less likely to find a mate.

_______ **4.** Tsetse flies kill animals by giving them the sleeping sickness.

Writing

A. Organize. Place each detail in the correct box.

a. each zebra has unique stripes
b. white stripes reflect heat
c. injuries break striped pattern
d. stripes confuse Tsetse fly
e. stripes look like tall grass
f. black stripes absorb heat

A Zebra's Stripes			
Camouflage	Identification	Mating	Temperature Control

B. Synthesize. Using Organize above, complete the conversation between a zebra researcher and a reporter.

Reporter: Why do zebras have stripes? Are they useful?

Researcher: We're not exactly sure why a zebra has stripes, but we do know some things they are used for; like ________, ________, ________ ________, and ________.

Reporter: Can you explain more?

Researcher: Sure. As ________, a zebra's stripes help it hide from lions in ________ ________. For ________, a zebra's stripes help tell others if it is healthy or weak. Also each zebra has ________ ________, so zebras are able to identify each other by them.

Reporter: What about temperature ________?

Researcher: Well, that is a bit too complicated to explain today, maybe next time!

UNIT 15

Instead of Us

Guesswork

Discuss your answers to these questions with your classmates.

1. What are the people in the picture doing?

2. What tools are they using? How are those tools helpful?

3. Why aren't they practicing on real people?

▲ Two people walking by a department store's window display of mannequins in New York City

Instead of Us

RH2-15
MP3

Have you ever had this strange experience? You are walking through a store, and out of the corner of your eye you see a person. You turn around to look, but it's just a big doll wearing clothes. These human dolls are called mannequins. Stores use them to display things like clothes, hats, and jewelry. Wearing clothes isn't the only thing they do well, though.

▲ Artist's mannequin

Mannequin comes from a Dutch word meaning, "little man." At first, mannequins were very small. Artists used

▲ One kind of mannequin is called a crash test dummy. The name explains most of what they do. Crash dummies help us make cars safer by testing what happens to people in car crashes.

▲ **1955 'Operation Teapot' atomic test** Operation Teapot was a series of fourteen nuclear test explosions conducted at the Nevada Test Site in the first half of 1955. Mannequins were placed in and around vehicles and buildings.

them as models of the human body. They are useful to artists because they can be moved into many different positions. Mannequins can also stay in one position forever. A real human would never last that long.

Mannequins have gotten bigger since then and are now used for a variety of things. They are useful in pretty much any training situation where a real person would be uncomfortable, or in danger. Rescue workers practice CPR on mannequins with mechanical lungs. They also practice saving mannequins from accidents, or from burning buildings.

Mannequins have also been used to test how humans will react to a nuclear explosion. They are placed in fake towns—at dinner tables, in cars, and at schools. A nuclear bomb is then detonated, and the mannequins are tested for radiation afterwards. Some nuclear test sites are still full of old mannequins.

Humans are glad that mannequins are so useful. No person wants to be the test subject for a nuclear explosion!

Vocabulary

A. Answer the questions in complete sentences. The first one has been done for you.

1. The restaurant displays its food in the front window. Does it cook or show the food there?

It shows the food there.

2. Knives are quite useful for cutting meat. Are they helpful or harmful?

____

3. Tom broke the vase. It was an accident. Did he mean to do it, or was it a mistake?

____

4. My new bed is very uncomfortable. Does it feel good or bad?

____

5. That painting is a fake. Is it real or not real?

____

6. Everyone was scared when he detonated the bomb. Did he set off the bomb or stop it?

____

B. Read the passage below. Match each phrase in red with its equivalent expression.

There are **a variety of** dangers that come with driving a car. People hope it won't **stay that way** forever, though. New technology makes cars safer and safer. Maybe someday your car will be able to protect you anytime you **are in danger**!

1. not change ________________
2. many different kinds of ________________
3. might be harmed ________________

Reading Comprehension

A. Main Ideas. Circle the answer that best completes each statement.

1. Mannequins are used in stores __________.

a. to display clothes **b.** as models for artists

2. The word mannequin came from a Dutch word meaning __________.

a. little man **b.** test subject

3. Mannequins are used for things that humans __________.

a. are more useful for **b.** can't, or don't want to do

B. Details. Write True or False or Not Given after each statement.

1. The first mannequins were useful because they could be moved around. __________

2. Mannequins are sometimes detonated to create nuclear explosions. __________

3. Real humans are sometimes used as artists' models. __________

4. Most mannequins look like big human dolls. __________

5. Rescue workers use mannequins for their training. __________

6. Radiated mannequins are left at nuclear test sites because they are dangerous. __________

C. Inferences. Decide which of the statements can be inferred from the passage. Check the correct answers. (Choose two.)

_______ **1.** Mannequins are useful for firefighters and police officers.

_______ **2.** Mannequins sometimes wear shoes and hold handbags.

_______ **3.** Mannequins have been around for hundreds of years.

_______ **4.** Rescue workers practice saving mannequins from nuclear explosions.

Writing

A. Organize. Place each detail in the correct box.

a. CPR practice
b. saved from burning buildings
c. saved from accidents
d. nuclear test subject
e. display clothes in store

The Many Uses of Mannequins	
Used because a real person would be...	**Use**
Uncomfortable	
In danger	

B. Synthesize. Using Organize above, complete the missing information and match each fact about mannequins with the correct picture.

1. Rescue workers use mannequins for __________ __________ and also practice saving them from __________ and __________ __________.

2. Mannequins are used in __________ to __________ clothes, jewelry, hats and other things.

3. Small mannequins are used by __________ as models of the human body.

4. Mannequins are used as __________ __________ for nuclear explosions.

16 UNIT

Stuck Together

Guesswork

Discuss your answers to these questions with your classmates.

1. What is the boy doing? Does it look like fun?
2. What is the black thing hanging over the wall?
3. Do you think the boy will stick to it?

▲ The name "Velcro" was made by combining the first three letters of two words — velvet and crochet.

▲ **Velcro** A special kind of temporary fastener that uses tiny hooks and loops to attach things together. It makes a loud ripping sound when it is pulled apart.

RH2-16
MP3

Stuck Together

Try this fun game. Run and jump at a wall. Can you stick to it? Don't try this on a regular wall — try it on an inflatable one. And don't forget to wear a suit! No, this isn't just a crazy game, and don't worry, nobody gets hurt. It's actually lots of fun. And it's all thanks to Velcro.

When George de Mestral invented Velcro, he thought it would soon replace buttons and zippers all over the world. He probably never thought that one day people would put on suits covered in Velcro and throw themselves at Velcro-covered walls. His invention isn't just used for fun and games, though. People have found incredible uses for Velcro all over Earth, and even in space.

▲ Velcro is used to attach things to the walls, ceiling, and even to astronauts in this space shuttle.

▲ A US flag attached to a soldier's uniform with Velcro

NASA uses over ten thousand square inches of Velcro in each of its space shuttles. It's all over the walls so that astronauts can attach tools, boxes, and even themselves to it. A small piece of Velcro is in each astronaut's helmet. They use it as a nose scratcher.

The Army uses Velcro on soldier's uniforms for their patches, and to hold their pockets closed. Their Velcro is special, though. It's silent. Don't ask them how they made it. It's a military secret!

Velcro is often used in children's clothing and shoes. It is much easier to use than buttons, zippers, or shoelaces. From kid's clothes to space, Velcro is everywhere. Who knows where it will show up next!

▲ NASA astronaut Gene Cernan is scratching his nose on a piece of Velcro inside his bubble helmet.

Vocabulary

A. Circle the correct answer and write it in the blank.

1. An inflatable object can be filled with ________. **a.** water **b.** air

2. A suit is clothing with a ________ purpose. **a.** special **b.** foreign

3. To invent is to ________ for the first time. **a.** create **b.** use

4. An astronaut is someone who travels in ________. **a.** the ocean **b.** space

5. If something is temporary it lasts for a ________ time. **a.** short **b.** long

6. A fastener is used to hold things ________. **a.** together **b.** apart

7. A pocket is used to ________ small items. **a.** clean **b.** hold

8. A uniform is a kind of ________ clothing. **a.** official **b.** expensive

9. A helmet is worn to ________ the head. **a.** shape **b.** protect

10. Shoelaces are used to ________ shoes. **a.** tie **b.** prevent

B. Choose the answer closest in meaning to the underlined part of the sentence.

1. Computers aren't just for fun and games. They have serious uses too.

a. competition **b.** entertainment

2. Do you think I can make this penny stick to the ceiling?

a. attach to **b.** go through

3. The success of this project is all thanks to Debra.

a. instead of **b.** because of

Reading Comprehension

A. Main Ideas. Circle the answer that best completes each statement.

1. Velcro is useful because it lets you __________.

a. move things together　　b. attach things together

2. Velcro is used in space to __________.

a. hold pockets close　　b. hold tools to walls

3. Velcro is useful for children because it is __________.

a. easy to use　　b. everywhere

B. Details. Write True or False or Not Given after each statement.

1. Velcro can be used underwater. __________

2. The inventor of Velcro thought it would be used instead of buttons. __________

3. People use Velcro to attach themselves to walls. __________

4. Astronauts use Velcro to scratch their helmets. __________

5. The military uses regular Velcro. __________

6. Children use Velcro to hold their shoes closed. __________

C. Inferences. Decide which of the statements can be inferred from the passage. Check the correct answers. (Choose three.)

_______ **1.** Astronauts cannot touch their noses when they are wearing a space suit.

_______ **2.** People sometimes jump from airplanes wearing Velcro-covered suits.

_______ **3.** Silent Velcro is useful in war because the enemy can't hear it.

_______ **4.** Buttons and zippers are difficult for small children to use.

Writing

A. Organize. Place each detail in the correct box.

- attach things to walls
- children's clothing and shoes
- uniform patches and pockets
- silent Velcro
- nose scratcher

Location	Usage of Velcro
Everyday Life	a. ______________________________
Space	a. ______________________________ b. ______________________________
Military	a. ______________________________ b. ______________________________

B. Synthesize. Using Organize above, complete the missing information in the conversation between George de Mestral and a reporter.

Reporter: When you invented __________, did you know how useful it would be?

Mestral: I had no idea how many things it would be used for.

Reporter: What surprised you the most?

Mestral: I was amazed when I found out Velcro was used in __________ to __________ things to space shuttle __________. They even use it as a __________ __________!

Reporter: Any other uses surprise you?

Mestral: I never expected that the military would invent __________ __________ to be used for their __________ __________ and __________.

17 UNIT

A Self-Portrait?

Guesswork

Discuss your answers to these questions with your classmates.

1. Do you recognize this painting? What is it called?
2. Do you notice anything special about this painting?
3. Who do you think this is a painting of?

▲ The Mona Lisa's eyes seem to follow you wherever you go, as if she is truly alive. Painters have tried to copy the effect, but have not had much success.

▲ Self-portrait of Leonardo da Vinci

RH2-17
MP3

A Self-Portrait?

The Mona Lisa is the most famous portrait in the world. It might also be the most mysterious. For decades, researchers have argued about who and what the painting shows. Most people believe it is a painting of Lisa del Giocondo. Some believe it is a portrait of the painter's mother, and others believe it is a self-portrait of the painter, Leonardo da Vinci!

Did You Know?

Lisa del Giocondo was a simple woman whose husband asked Leonardo to paint her portrait. Many people think the Mona Lisa is this portrait.

◀ **Mona Lisa painting** (left) **at the Louvre museum** (right) **in Paris, France**
Since Mona Lisa started gaining fame in the 1900's it has been stolen, damaged by a rock, and even had a teacup thrown at it. For these reasons it is now protected by bullet-proof glass.

The painting shows a woman sitting in a chair and looking outwards. She is smiling mysteriously. Because of her smile, some people think she is hiding something. These people have great fun trying to guess the secret of the Mona Lisa's smile.

The secret might be Leonardo's great joke. One researcher noticed some similarities between Leonardo's self-portrait and the Mona Lisa. She was curious, so she compared the two with a computer. The two faces match up perfectly! Did Leonardo paint himself as a woman? Some researchers think so. Others think that the portrait looks like Leonardo because it is actually a portrait of his mother.

Leonardo's mother was dead by the time that he painted her portrait. He could have used his own face as a model for the painting. It is hard to tell whether he meant for the painting to look like him, or whether it just happened. But it is clear that he took the painting very seriously. He spent 15 years of his life working on it!

Vocabulary

A. **Answer the questions in complete sentences. The first one has been done for you.**

1. Rembrandt was a famous portrait painter. Did he paint people or landscapes?

He painted people.

2. It took the author a decade to finish that novel. Did it take him 5 years or 10 years?

____

3. My parents often argue about money. Do they agree or disagree?

____

4. Watch out, that door opens outwards. Does it open towards the outside or the inside?

____

5. There are many similarities between America and Canada. Are they alike or unlike?

____

6. The painter's real identity is a secret. Is it known or unknown?

____

B. **Read the sentences. Circle the best definition for each underlined word.**

1. I used our house as a model for my school art project.

a. as an example **b.** as a process

2. I love watching Marie play ping pong because she takes it so seriously.

a. doesn't think much about it **b.** considers it to be important

3. I heard that you are working on writing a new book.

a. busy with **b.** tired from

Reading Comprehension

A. Main Ideas. Circle the answer that best completes each statement.

1. Researchers argue about __________ .

a. who made the Mona Lisa
b. who is shown in the Mona Lisa

2. The Mona Lisa's secret might be that __________ .

a. Leonardo painted himself in the portrait
b. Leonardo's mother painted the portrait

B. Details. Circle the answers that best complete each statement.

1. Because Leonardo's portrait and the Mona Lisa (1) __________ , researchers think (2) __________ .

(1) **a.** match together **b.** are portraits
c. were painted by Leonardo

(2) **a.** they are famous **b.** Leonardo painted them both
c. they are of the same person

2. The portrait might be of Leonardo's dead (1) __________ , and Leonardo might have used (2) __________ as a model.

(1) **a.** mother **b.** wife **c.** secret

(2) **a.** his own face **b.** Lisa del Giocondo **c.** his painting

C. Inferences. Decide which of the statements can be inferred from the passage. Check the correct answers. (Choose one.)

_______ **1.** Leonardo da Vinci was really a woman.

_______ **2.** Leonardo knew that the Mona Lisa would become world famous.

_______ **3.** Leonardo cared deeply about the Mona Lisa.

_______ **4.** Lisa del Giocondo helped Leonardo paint the Mona Lisa.

Writing

A. Organize. Place each detail in the correct box.

- The Mona Lisa is a self-portrait of Leonardo da Vinci.
- The Mona Lisa is a portrait of Leonardo's mother.
- The woman in the painting is smiling mysteriously.
- Researchers are still arguing about who and what the painting shows.

Theory	Supporting ideas
The Mona Lisa might be hiding something.	____________________ ____________________
____________________ ____________________	His portrait and the Mona Lisa match up perfectly.
____________________ ____________________	Because his mother was dead, he might have used his own face as a model for the painting.
Mona Lisa might be the most mysterious painting in the world.	____________________ ____________________

B. Synthesize. Using Organize above, complete the conversation between the Mona Lisa researcher and a reporter.

Reporter: When did you first think that the Mona Lisa was __________ something?

Researcher: As soon as I saw the woman's __________ smile.

Reporter: And then you found that Leonardo's __________ matches up perfectly with the ______________?

Researcher: Yes. It made me think that it is really a __________________ of Leonardo.

Reporter: Do you have any other theories?

Researcher: Yes. I think it could also be a portrait of Leonardo's __________.

18 UNIT

What Is Art?

Guesswork

Discuss your answers to these questions with your classmates.

1. What does this look like to you?

2. Do you think this is art? Why or why not?

3. What makes something art?

▲ A side-view of "The Physical Impossibility of Death in the Mind of Someone Living" by Damien Hirst, in the Metropolitan Museum of Art in New York City

RH2-18
MP3

What Is Art?

Art is beautiful, right? Art is painting, drawing, and sculpting. But is that all? Marcel Duchamp didn't think so. In 1917 he displayed an incredible new "artwork." It was a men's urinal that he turned upside down and signed with a fake name. Many art critics were disgusted, but the art world embraced his new idea of what "art"was. Nowadays it seems like anything can be art.

Found Object Art

How much would you pay for a dead shark? Not much? Well, Steven Cohen paid $8 million for one. It wasn't just

▲ Banksy Graffiti: (from left) Chinatown, New York City; Camden Town, London; Liverpool, England

any dead shark, though. It was a piece of art made by Damien Hirst. Hirst caught a shark and then preserved it in a clear box filled with green liquid. Many people complained that it wasn't real art, but it's hard to argue with an $8 million price tag. Something that expensive must be art!

▲ Bregenz, Austria: Damien Hirst's shark, preserved in formaldehyde at an exhibition of art objects

Graffiti art

Anyone caught spray-painting on a public building is usually arrested or fined. Police call them vandals. But there is one vandal who is safe from the police, even though he has spray-painted on buildings all over the world. He calls himself Banksy, and he is a graffiti artist. His art is so popular that usually no one washes it away.

Performance art

Performance artists are special. They don't just make art, they do it. One performance artist even lived in a glass house for a few months. People could watch everything she did. Her life became art.

▲ Israeli artist Lital Dotan in "The Glasshouse," San Francisco; Passers-by can watch through the windows as the artist gets dressed, eats, practices yoga and makes art.

Vocabulary

A. Circle the answer that fits best with the word in red.

1. sculpting	clay / water / air
2. sign	thought / idea / name
3. embrace	take / accept / give
4. preserve	take / give / keep
5. urinal	bathroom / living room / kitchen
6. complain	pleased / unhappy / respected
7. spray-paint	can / bottle / cup
8. fine	jail / money / beating
9. vandal	criminal / actor / adult
10. arrest	judge / lawyer / police

B. Complete the sentences by choosing the correct answer.

1. I turned the book upside down, so the bottom is facing ________ now.

a. upwards **b.** downwards

2. It seems like Corey really likes that girl. It's ________ that he likes her.

a. definite **b.** possible

3. Mom told you to wash away that dirt. You should ________ before she gets home.

a. clean it up **b.** send it away

Reading Comprehension

A. Main Ideas. Complete the statement by circling the correct choice for each blank.

The passage is mainly about the **1.** __________ of **2.** __________. So the main idea is that **3.** __________.

1. a. different kinds b. expensive kinds

2. a. performance art b. modern art

3. a. some kinds of modern art can be very expensive
b. modern art takes many different forms

B. Details. Write True or False or Not Given after each statement.

1. Marcel Duchamp created art out of a men's urinal. __________

2. Damien Hirst paid $8 million for a dead shark in a box. __________

3. Everybody believed that Damien Hirst's dead shark was a great artwork. __________

4. Graffiti artists are sometimes arrested for spray-painting on buildings. __________

5. Performance artists sometimes live in glass houses for many years. __________

6. Banksy creates art with spray-paint. __________

C. Inferences. Decide which of the statements can be inferred from the passage. Check the correct answers. (Choose two.)

_______ **1.** Marcel Duchamp's urinal artwork was an important piece of art.

_______ **2.** It cost Damien Hirst millions of dollars to catch the shark and preserve it.

_______ **3.** There are more kinds of art now than there were in the past.

_______ **4.** Banksy uses a fake name because police all over the world are trying to catch him.

Writing

A. Organize. Place each fact or term in the correct box.

- Don't just make art, do it
- Illegal
- $8 million
- Done on public buildings
- Banksy
- A shark preserved in a box
- Damien Hirst
- Lived in a glass house for a few months

Modern Art	
Performance Art	a. ______________________
	b. ______________________
Graffiti Art	a. ______________________
	b. ______________________
	c. ______________________
Found Object Art	a. ______________________
	b. ______________________
	c. ______________________

B. Synthesize. Using Organize above, complete the blanks in this interview between a reporter and an art critic.

Reporter: Can you tell me a bit about modern art?

Art critic: Modern art takes many different forms. One of the most expensive is Damien Hirst's __________ __________. It sold for __________.

Reporter: Wow. That's a lot of money. What other kinds of modern art are popular?

Art critic: Banksy's __________ art is incredibly popular. Even though it is __________, many cities allow it to stay on their __________.

Art critic: There's also performance art. These artists don't just __________ art, they do it.

UNIT 19

Human Lightning Rod

Guesswork

Discuss your answers to these questions with your classmates.

1. What is the man holding? What do you think might happen?

2. Do you think there is a chance the man could be struck by lightning?

3. Have you ever been struck by lightning?

RH2-19
MP3

Human Lightning Rod

▲ Roy's seventh lightning strike earned him a place in the Guinness Book of World Records. It was an honor he would have preferred not to earn.

Lightning strikes fairly often, but it rarely strikes people. The chance of being struck once in your life is 1/6,000. The chance of being struck twice is about the same as winning the lottery: 1/36,000,000. Roy Sullivan was struck by lightning seven times. If his bad luck had been good luck, he might have become a billionaire.

▲ Roy Sullivan was a park ranger at Shenandoah National Park. On seven occasions between 1942 and 1977, six of them in the park, Ranger Sullivan was struck by lightning.

▲ Right before he was struck for the sixth time, Roy saw a storm cloud. He tried running away, but the lighting hit him before he could escape.

All seven strikes occurred while Roy worked as a park ranger in Shenandoah National Park. The first was in 1942, during a severe thunderstorm. The lightning bolt burned a strip down his right leg and left a hole in his shoe.

The next strike was in 1969. This one knocked him unconscious and burned off his eyebrows, eyelashes, and most of his hair. Roy survived two more strikes in the next two years, but he began to believe he was cursed. He now kept a can of water with him at all times.

One day in 1973 Roy's caution paid off. After fleeing from a dark storm cloud in his truck, Roy decided he was safe. He got out of the vehicle and was immediately struck by lightning. It knocked off his shoe and set his hair on fire. He just grabbed the can of water and poured it over his head.

By the time he died in 1983, Roy had been struck twice more. The last strike happened when he was fishing. After Roy was struck, a bear tried to steal his trout. Roy wasn't worried. He scared the bear away with a stick!

Vocabulary

A. Answer the questions in complete sentences. The first one has been done for you.

1. I rarely eat broccoli. Do I eat it often or not very often?

You don't eat it very often.

2. My father won the lottery! Did he win a sports competition or a game?

____

3. A strange event occurred last night. Did it happen or end?

____

4. There was a severe storm last night. Was the storm strong or weak?

____

5. Dan fell off the ladder and was unconscious when we found him. Was he awake or asleep?

____

6. Beth died immediately after hitting the ground. Did she die right away or after some time?

____

B. Fill in the blanks using the expressions from the box.

knocked off	scare away	on fire

1. If you play with lighters you might set your house ________________ .

2. If we act big and loud we might be able to ________________ the bear.

3. The explosion was so big that it ________________ my shoes and sent my hat flying.

Reading Comprehension

A. Main Ideas. Circle the correct answer to the question.

1. What is the main idea of this passage?

a. Roy Sullivan was very unlucky.
b. Roy Sullivan was a park ranger.
c. Roy Sullivan did not die of a lightning strike.
d. Roy Sullivan could have become a billionaire.

B. Details. Complete each sentence with the correct answer.

1. The 2nd lightning strike __________ .

a. burned off Roy's eyebrows
b. knocked his shoe off
c. burned a strip down his right leg

2. Roy planned on using the can of water to __________ .

a. prevent the lightning from striking him
b. put out any fires if he was struck again
c. help him flee from the lightning

C. Inferences. Decide which of the statements can be inferred from the passage. Check the correct answers. (Choose two.)

_______ **1.** Roy's second and third lightning strikes happened while he was a park ranger.

_______ **2.** Roy Sullivan was scared of thunderstorms.

_______ **3.** Roy Sullivan could predict when he would be struck by lightning.

_______ **4.** Lighting often strikes people more than once.

Writing

A. Organize. Write each answer (a-h) in the correct box.

a. knocked unconscious
b. knocked off shoe
c. struck while fishing
d. Roy poured water over his head
e. burned a strip down right leg
f. set eyebrows on fire
g. left a hole in shoe
h. Roy started keeping a can of water with him

When Lightning Strikes!			
1st STRIKE	2nd STRIKE	3rd~5th STRIKE	7th STRIKE

B. Synthesize. Using Organize above, complete the missing information. Be careful to use the correct tense.

1	Roy starts working as a __________ __________ at Shenandoah National Park.
2	Lightning strikes Roy and __________ __________ __________ __________ his leg.
3	Roy is left __________ by a lightning strike.
4	Roy starts carrying __________ __________ __________ __________ with him at all times.
5	Lightning __________ __________ his shoe and sets his hair on fire.
6	Roy is struck by lightning while __________.

GLOBE FIRE DESCENDING INTO A ROOM.

UNIT 20

A Shocking Sight

Guesswork

Discuss your answers to these questions with your classmates.

1. What is happening in the picture?

2. What do you think the ball is made of? Where did it come from?

3. What do you think will happen to the people in the room?

▲ From top: ball lightning, cloud to ground lightning, cloud-to-cloud lightning

RH2-20
MP3

A Shocking Sight

When you think of lightning, do you imagine long streaks of light shooting from the sky? This is the most common kind of lightning. It's not the only kind, though. For hundreds of years there have been stories of a rare, slow-moving, ball-shaped kind of lightning. Until recently, scientists thought these stories were just hoaxes or fantasy. Now they have explanations for what ball lightning might be.

One of the earliest stories of ball lightning comes from 1638. An 8-foot-wide ball of fire entered a church during a huge thunderstorm. The ball knocked stones off of the walls, destroyed pews and windows, and smelled badly of sulfur. Ball lightning is described differently in other stories. Sometimes it strikes people and kills them. Other times people are struck, but they say it only tingles. The most dramatic kinds of ball lightning explode with a loud bang, killing people and destroying buildings.

Scientists have all kinds of explanations for this phenomenon. One of the most unusual is that ball lightning isn't lightning at all. They say that it is actually miniature black holes traveling through the sky. Other scientists have an incredible explanation. They discovered that regular lightning affects our brains when it strikes very close by. These scientists think that a close strike of

▲ **Simulated view of a black hole** Scientists believe that miniature black holes were created at the same time as the universe. Because of their unique origins, miniature black holes are much smaller than normal and will probably last forever.

lightning can cause us to think that we are seeing floating circles. So ball lightning might just be a kind of fantasy after all!

Did You Know?

People have discovered that you can create a strange kind of floating light in your microwave at home. Some scientists think it may be the same thing as ball lightning.

Vocabulary

A. Circle the correct answer and write it in the blank.

1. A streak is shaped like a ________ . **a.** circle **b.** line

2. A common idea is known by ________ people. **a.** many **b.** few

3. A hoax is a kind of ________ . **a.** trick **b.** party

4. A pew is a place to ________ . **a.** sit **b.** stand

5. A church is a place for ________ . **a.** religion **b.** business

6. A fantasy is a(n) ________ story. **a.** real **b.** imagined

7. Sulfur is a yellow chemical that smells ________ . **a.** good **b.** bad

8. To shoot is to move ________ . **a.** slowly **b.** quickly

9. A phenomenon is a ________ event. **a.** special **b.** typical

10. To be dramatic is to be very ________ . **a.** extreme **b.** boring

B. Fill in the blanks using the expressions from the box.

other times	until recently	after all

1. ________________, I thought you were my friend. Now I know better!

2. I can't believe you were lying to me ________________. I should have trusted Eric.

3. Sometimes I think we will love each other forever. ________________, I'm not so sure.

Reading Comprehension

A. Main Ideas. Circle the best answer to the question.

1. What is this passage mainly about?

a. the effects of ball lightning
b. the movement of ball lightning
c. dangers and fantasies of ball lightning
d. descriptions and theories about ball lightning

B. Details. Write True or False or Not Given after each statement.

1. Ball lightning struck a church in 1368. ________

2. Ball lightning isn't always dangerous. ________

3. Ball lightning has killed thousands of people. ________

4. Sometimes ball lightning explodes. ________

5. People see ball lightning often during thunderstorms. ________

6. Miniature black holes may make us imagine that we see balls of light. ________

C. Inferences. Decide which of the statements can be inferred from the passage. Check the correct answers. (Choose two.)

______ **1.** Most reports of ball lightning were probably hoaxes.

______ **2.** Ball lightning can be very dangerous.

______ **3.** Ball lightning may be able to create miniature black holes.

______ **4.** Lightning can affect our vision.

Writing

A. Organize. Place each fact in the correct box.

a. miniature black holes may be responsible for ball lightning
b. rare
c. knocks stones off walls
d. kills people
e. regular lightning causes us to see floating circles
f. slow-moving
g. destroys buildings
h. close strikes of regular lightning affect our brains
i. ball-shaped

Ball Lightning		
Effects	**Description**	**Explanations**

B. Synthesize. Using Organize above, complete blanks in this overview of a meeting of the International Committee on Ball Lightning.

10th Meeting of the International Committee on Ball Lightning

Directive: To discuss the characteristics and causes of ________ ________

Known facts

Description: a ________ kind of ________-moving, ball-________ lightning

Effects: known to ________ buildings and ________ people, but sometimes is harmless

Current Theories: could be miniature ________ ________ traveling through the sky, or images caused by close-by strikes of ________ lightning

CREDITS

Photo Credits: **Page 5** Wikimedia Commons; **Page 6** Wikipedia; **Page 7** Martin Pettitt/Flickr; **Page 11** Wikipedia; **Page 13** (top left) efteling.com, (top right) Wikipedia, (middle, bottom) Wikimedia Commons; **Page 16** Wikimedia Commons; **Page 17** Pierre Holtz-UNICEF; **Page 18** (top left) Rob Rogoyski/Flickr, (top right) Wikipedia; **Page 19** (top left) Flickr, (top right) EBKauai/Flickr; **Page 22** Flickr; **Page 23** Shutterstock; **Page 24** Nick Harris/Flickr, Brian Mckay/Flickr, Tambako/Flickr, Jonny Hughes/Flickr, Stuard Richards/Flickr, Kevin Law/Flickr; **Page 25** Wikipedia; **Page 28** Wikipedia; **Page 29** Simon Cast/Flickr; **Page 30** (top) Olivier Lejade/Flickr, (bottom) JackyR/Wikimedia Commons; **Page 31** (top) hannes.steyn/Flickr, (bottom) Nachoman-au/Wikimedia Commons; **Page 35** (top) McKay Savage/Flickr, (bottom) L. Shyamal/Wikimedia Commons; **Page 36** Shutterstock; **Page 37** (top left) Shutterstock, (top right) Forz/Wikimedia Commons, (bottom) Wikimedia Commons; **Page 41** Michael Warren/Flickr; **Page 42** (top) Phil Shaw/Wikimedia commons, (middle) eukonkanto.fi, (bottom) Michael Warren/Flickr; **Page 43** Nick Holland/Flickr; **Page 47** Shutterstock; **Page 48** Shutterstock; **Page 49** (top left) Leigh Caldwell/Flickr, (top right) Brad Gocken/Wikimedia Commons; **Page 52** Wikimedia Commons; **Page 53** Curtsey of Brooke Greenberg family; **Page 54** Curtsey of Brooke Greenberg family; **Page 55** Curtsey of Brooke Greenberg family; **Page 58** Curtsey of Brooke Greenberg family; **Page 59** Flickr; **Page 60** (top) Bob Garrard, (bottom) Kevin King/Flickr; **Page 61** U.S. Federal Government; **Page 64** Wikipedia; **Page 65** Boston Public Library; **Page 66** (top left) Jon Petitti/Flickr, (top right) Boston Public Library, (bottom) Wikipedia; **Page 67** Boston Public Library; **Page 71** Alan Wu/Flickr; **Page 73** Wikimedia Commons; **Page 76** (top left) Flickr, (middle) Wikimedia Commons, (top right) United Nations Development, (bottom left) Cameron Strandberg/Flickr, (bottom right) Flickr; **Page 77** IPMIMAGES; **Page 78** (top left) Jasper Nance/Flickr, (top right) Wikipedia; **Page 79** (top) David P. Hughes, (middle) Clemson University/IPMIMAGES, (bottom) Randy Cyr/IPMIMAGES; **Page 82** Shutterstock; **Page 83** Wikimedia Commons; **Page 84** Brandon Daniel/Flickr; **Page 85** (top) Shutterstock, (middle) Flickr, (bottom) Arno Meintjes NC/Flickr; **Page 88** Brandon Daniel/Flickr; **Page 89** Flickr; **Page 90** (top) Flick, (bottom) Shutterstock; **Page 91** (left, middle) Wikimedia Commons, (right) James Vaughan/Flickr; **Page 94** (from left) Gerald Davison/Flickr, Sharilyn Neidhardt/Flickr, wez/Flickr, James Vaughan/Flickr; **Page 95** Brian Suda/Flickr; **Page 96** (top left) Flickr, (top right) Wikipedia; **Page 97** (top left) NASA, (top right) Joakim Fjeldli/Flickr, (bottom) NASA; **Page 101** Wikipedia; **Page 102** Wikipedia; **Page 103** (top left) Roger Wo/Flickr, (top right) Flickr, (bottom) Picasa; **Page 107** Micha L. Rieser/Flickr; **Page 108** Andrew Brannan/Flickr; **Page 109** (top left) Wikimedia Commons, (top middle) Michael Summers/Flickr, (top right) Klara Kim/Flickr, (middle) Flickr, (bottom) Lital Dotan & Eyal Perry; **Page 113** dalecottam/Flickr; **Page 114** Wikipedia; **Page 115** (left) Dave Fulmer/Flickr, (right) Gary Robertson/Flickr; **Page 119** Wikipedia; **Page 120** (top) Storm Wolf/Flickr, (middle) Wikimedia Commons, (bottom) Wikimedia Commons; **Page 121** (top) Wikipedia, (bottom) Flickr

Illustration Credit: Won Yoo Sung

Notes

Notes

Notes

Enriching the Mind through Intriguing Learning-Oriented Readings

Reading Highlights

2

Workbook

WorldCom Edu

Reading Highlights

2

Workbook

WorldCom ELT

UNIT 01

From Fiction to Fact

Words & Expressions

A. Choose the correct definition for each word below.

fantastic	probably	eventually	suggest	mysterious

1. ________________: to say what you think is true, or should happen
2. ________________: having a strong chance of being true, or happening
3. ________________: amazing and wonderful
4. ________________: after some time
5. ________________: strange and hard to understand

B. Choose the word that best completes each sentence.

1. I watched a funny, modern ________ of the story of Beowulf.
   a. shaft b. fairy c. diet d. version

2. We buried our dog's body deep ________ so wild animals couldn't eat it.
   a. underground b. within c. behind d. above water

3. I dropped my baseball down the mine ________. I don't think I'll ever see it again.
   a. diet b. shaft c. orphan d. fairy tale

C. Fill in the blanks using the expressions from the box.

care for	as a sign	ran away

1. People need to ________________ their pets.
2. Yesterday my dog ________________, but today he came back.
3. Some people see strange weather ________________ that global warming is real.

Summary

D. Complete the summary with the correct words.

green beans	children	died	orphans	lost

A folk tale tells of two green-skinned ____________ who appeared in Woolpit, England one day. They couldn't speak English and only ate ____________. One ____________ soon, but the other survived and eventually ____________ her green color. Once she learned English, she explained that she came from another world. There is a more realistic explanation, though. One modern historian thinks the children were actually ____________ who became lost in the forest.

Writing

E. Unscramble the words and write them in the blanks.

1. that were designed / discovered them / to trap wolves / villagers / in old pits

____.

2. the children / died / after their parents / who ran away / were orphans

____.

3. they / survived / vegetables / by eating / in the forest

____.

F. Look at the picture and answer the question. Use the hint in the parenthesis.

Q. What is she doing? **(wand)**

➡ ____

________________________.

UNIT 02

Real Enough

Words & Expressions

A. Choose the correct definition for each word below.

address	sink	matter	sail	mistaken

1. ________________ : wrong about something
2. ________________ : to go down into a liquid
3. ________________ : to be important
4. ________________ : the name of the place that a building or person is located
5. ________________ : to move by wind power

B. Choose the word that best completes each sentence.

1. When there is lightning you should find ________ in a building.

   a. sailors b. crews c. omens d. safety

2. Don't bother me or I might ________ this car!

   a. sink b. frighten c. address d. crash

3. All of the passengers on that plane knew that they were ________ to die.

   a. addressed b. accepted c. doomed d. safe

C. Fill in the blanks using the expressions from the box.

until the end of time	to this day	as the legend goes

1. ________________, the children never made it back out of the woods.
2. ________________, I still don't like driving my car under that bridge.
3. I promise I will love you ________________.

Summary

D. Complete the summary with the correct words.

bad luck	sank	sail	sailors	curse

In 1614 a ship ____________ off the Cape of Good Hope. Legend says that its captain screamed a ____________ as he went down into the sea. ____________ claim that the ship is still trying to ____________ around the Cape. They say that seeing the Flying Dutchman is ____________, and could even get you killed.

Writing

E. Unscramble the words and write them in the blanks.

1. a Dutch ship / the Cape of Good Hope, / was trying / when it / to make it around / sank

____.

2. fought for hours / the ship / he and his crew / back to safety / to sail

____.

3. to accept one / any sailor / to die soon / foolish enough / was doomed

____.

F. Read the question and arrange the words into a complete and correct answer.

Q. What does this picture show?
(an illusion / how / could / the Flying Dutchman / have been)

➡ It shows ________________________________
________________________.

03 UNIT A Bright Idea

Words & Expressions

A. Choose the correct definition for each word below.

thirst	stranded	tinfoil	giant	pool

1. ________________ : the feeling of wanting water
2. ________________ : a place where water gathers
3. ________________ : a flexible, shiny metal
4. ________________ : incredibly large
5. ________________ : trapped somewhere like the desert or an island

B. Choose the word that best completes each sentence.

1. Straws and chewing gum were the only ________ that I used for my science project.
   a. diarrhea　　b. materials　　c. pots　　d. pools

2. Can you ________ this clay into a person?
   a. contaminate　　b. dehydrate　　c. shape　　d. strand

3. This ________ teaches you about the movement of water.
   a. material　　b. solar cooker　　c. diarrhea　　d. experiment

C. Fill in the blanks using the expressions from the box.

all you need	make a fire	in direct sunlight

1. Plants grow best ________________.
2. Making peanut butter is easy. ________________ is peanuts, a blender, and oil!
3. Did you know you can ________________ with a magnifying glass?

Summary

D. Complete the summary with the correct words.

save	bacteria	contaminated	pasteurize	solar cookers

____________ water can make you very sick, and can even kill you. ____________ can help. One kind is made from cardboard, tinfoil, a pot and a plastic bag. It uses the heat of the sun to ____________ the water, killing most disease-causing ____________. This cheap and easy to use technology could ____________ millions of lives around the world.

Writing

E. Unscramble the words and write them in the blanks.

1. drink from / the water is / that many animals / in a pool

____.

2. shape / and cover / a giant bowl, / the cardboard into / with tinfoil / the inside

____.

3. nearly / die from / contaminated water / two million children / drinking

____.

F. Read the question and arrange the words into a complete and correct answer.

Q. How does this solar cooker work?
(a pot / sunlight / to focus / shiny metal / onto)

➡ It uses ____
____________________________.

04 UNIT

What Do You See?

Words & Expressions

A. Choose the correct definition for each word below.

shade	trail	allow	dive	hawk

1. ________________ : a kind of bird that is good at hunting
2. ________________ : to go down suddenly
3. ________________ : to let happen or give permission
4. ________________ : a darker or lighter version of a color
5. ________________ : a path made by creatures

B. Choose the word that best completes each sentence.

1. That dog has been ________ the park for hours. Is it lost?

   a. bouncing b. detecting c. shading d. circling

2. I have a ________ telescope. I can see Jupiter!

   a. marine b. ultraviolet c. vision d. long-distance

3. Our house has a ________ problem. I can hear them scratching in the walls.

   a. rodent b. combination c. brain d. talon

C. Fill in the blanks using the expressions from the box.

on the other hand	for one thing	reached out

1. Jack ________________ and grabbed the oyster.
2. My mom makes great cookies. ________________, her brownies aren't very good.
3. Dogs make great pets. ________________ they are very loyal.

Summary

D. Complete the summary with the correct words.

color	birds	ultraviolet light	combination	different

Light bounces off of different things in ____________ ways. Your brain sees these differences as ____________. Human brains can see three main colors. Every other color is a ____________ of these three. ____________ can see four main colors. This allows them to see ____________ — a color that humans cannot see.

Writing

E. Unscramble the words and write them in the blanks.

1. hawks can / can't / see colors / that humans

____!

2. our brains see / color is / different kinds / the way that / of light

____.

3. an important color / is called / see / ultraviolet light / that birds can

____.

F. Read the question and arrange the words into a complete and correct answer.

Q. How many colors can a human being see?
(colors / see / more / ten million / than / can)

➡ A human being ______________________________
______________________________.

05 UNIT The Tree of Life

Words & Expressions

A. Choose the correct definition for each word below.

massive	hollow	house	shelter	fuel

1. ________________ : something that provides energy
2. ________________ : a place that protects you from the weather
3. ________________ : very large
4. ________________ : empty on the inside
5. ________________ : to provide a home

B. Choose the word that best completes each sentence.

1. I like to ________ the juice out of oranges.

   a. house b. suck c. consider d. fuel

2. We ________ our bikes under the porch during the winter.

   a. regenerate b. provide c. store d. consider

3. ________ protects a tree from injury.

   a. Fibers b. Bark c. Malaria d. Grain

C. Fill in the blanks using the expressions from the box.

known as	make sense	up to

1. On my baseball team I am ________________ "Slugger."
2. I can hold ________________ 20 marshmallows in my mouth at a time.
3. It doesn't ________________ that you became president. I've been here for much longer!

Summary

D. Complete the summary with the correct words.

droughts	storage	leaves	nutritious	bark

Baobab trees have many uses. Their fruit is ____________ and can be made into drinks, soups and porridges. Their trunks store lots of water that people can drink during ____________. Their trunks can also provide ____________ space. Their ____________ can be used to make clothes, rope and other things, and their ____________ protect against disease.

Writing

E. Unscramble the words and write them in the blanks.

1. quite as / no tree / is / as the Baobab / useful

____.

2. natives use / directly out of / hollow grass / to suck / the tree / water

____.

3. provides / to make cloth / be used / the bark / fibers that can

____.

F. Look at the picture and answer the question. Use the hint in the parenthesis.

Q. What does the picture show? **(in front of)**

➡ It shows a woman ________________________________

________________________.

UNIT 06

Not So Innocent

Words & Expressions

A. Choose the correct definition for each word below.

upwards	fig	entire	merge	single

1. ________________ : all of something
2. ________________ : to come together into one
3. ________________ : one by itself
4. ________________ : towards the sky
5. ________________ : a kind of tree that makes a pinkish fruit

B. Choose the word that best completes each sentence.

1. Let's have lunch in the ________ under that tree.

   a. stem b. merchandise c. branch d. shade

2. When you dig up weeds, make sure you get the ________ too.

   a. gardens b. roots c. merchants d. merchandise

3. There are 2,000 different plants in the ________ garden.

   a. murderous b. innocent c. botanical d. trunk

C. Fill in the blanks using the expressions from the box.

due to	known by	send out

1. Jack is ________________ a strange nickname. People call him Cheddar.
2. The store has to close ________________ poor sales.
3. We need to ________________ new invitations to the wedding.

Summary

D. Complete the summary with the correct words.

trunks	seeds	roots	trees	ground

The banyan tree is unlike most other trees. Instead of growing from the ground, it grows on other ______________ . Birds drop banyan ______________ on their branches, and the seeds send ______________ down to the ______________ . As the branches grow out, they send more roots down to the ground, and these roots become ______________ . In this way, a single banyan tree can take over an entire forest.

Writing

E. Unscramble the words and write them in the blanks.

1. as its name / the banyan isn't / makes it / as innocent / sound

____ .

2. a banyan seed / sprouts / a bird drops / and the seed / onto a branch,

____ .

3. due to / the original trunk / removed / disease / had to be

____ .

F. Read the question and arrange the words into a complete and correct answer.

Q. What is shown here?
(the roots / of / another tree / a banyan tree / are covering)

➡ ____
______________________________ .

UNIT 07

Just for Fun

Words & Expressions

A. Choose the correct definition for each word below.

method	iron	Finland	contestant	several

1. ________________ : being more than two or three but not many
2. ________________ : a way of doing something
3. ________________ : someone who participates in a competition
4. ________________ : a hot piece of metal used to flatten cloth
5. ________________ : a country in northern Europe

B. Choose the word that best completes each sentence.

1. Are you a(n) ________ in this race as well?

   a. method b. competitor c. wheel d. award

2. My brother and I loved ________ down that hill when we were kids.

   a. ironing b. struggling c. holding d. tumbling

3. When the cars crashed together, a ________ came off and rolled towards us.

   a. snowboard b. participant c. wheel d. parachute

C. Fill in the blanks using the expressions from the box.

in the middle of	take a look at	end up

1. Don't just stand ________________ the street. You're going to get hit!
2. Every time I eat at McDonald's, I ________________ feeling sick.
3. Please, ________________ my cat. I think he might be sick.

Summary

D. Complete the summary with the correct words.

ironing	statues	competitions	obstacle	wheel

People participate in all sorts of strange ____________. In a wife-carrying race, competitors carry their wives through an ____________ course. In Gloucester, England contestants chase a large ____________ of cheese down a steep hill. ____________ has become a sport too. People have ironed in canoes, on top of large ____________, while snowboarding and under the ice of a frozen lake.

Writing

E. Unscramble the words and write them in the blanks.

1. upside down / hang / most racers / off of their backs / have their wives

____.

2. stays on / the hill is / that nobody ever / so steep / their feet

____.

3. under the ice / participants / lake / have ironed / of a frozen

____.

F. Read the question and arrange the words into a complete and correct answer.

Q. What is happening in the picture?
(course / carrying / an obstacle / through / his wife)

➡ A man is ____
____________________________.

08
UNIT

Fame and Fortune

Words & Expressions

A. Choose the correct definition for each word below.

magician	talented	feature	quality	viewer

1. ____________ : someone who performs magic tricks
2. ____________ : to show in a main place
3. ____________ : having great ability and skill
4. ____________ : a measure of how good or bad a thing is
5. ____________ : someone who watches something

B. Choose the word that best completes each sentence.

1. My pencil is not very high ________. It always breaks.
   a. pop b. quality c. entertainment d. fame

2. Her singing was so ________ that I had to leave the concert hall.
   a. entertaining b. off-key c. quality d. talented

3. It was so ________ when I peed my pants that I hid it in the bathroom for the rest of the day.
   a. embarrassing b. amazing c. hidden d. complete

C. Fill in the blanks using the expressions from the box.

tried out for	make lots of money	their fair share of

1. Even doctors make ____________ mistakes.
2. When I grow up, I'm going to be a lawyer and ____________.
3. Sally ____________ the cheerleading team, but she didn't make it.

Summary

D. Complete the summary with the correct words.

try out	normal	wealthy	talents	funny

Idol shows offer a chance for ____________ people to become famous and ____________. Anybody can ____________ for them. Even bad singers become famous sometimes. Audiences love to watch idol shows. Great performances are fun to watch, and bad performances are often very ____________. Now new kinds of idol shows try to find hidden ____________, like juggling, sword-eating, and others.

Writing

E. Unscramble the words and write them in the blanks.

1. it doesn't / a good singer / even matter / if you are / or not

____.

2. their hidden / idol shows / to discover / aim / talents

____.

3. are the same / pop concerts / high quality / some performances / as professional

____.

F. Read the question and arrange the words into a complete and correct answer.

Q. What does this picture show?
(Michael Jackson, / shows / pop star / famous / a)

➡ It ____
______________________________.

09 UNIT Forever Young?

Words & Expressions

A. Choose the correct definition for each word below.

rate	discover	age	explain	condition

1. ____________________ : to get older
2. ____________________ : to tell why something is, or how it works
3. ____________________ : the state that a person or thing is in
4. ____________________ : a measure of how fast or slow something happens
5. ____________________ : to find for the first time

B. Choose the answer with the same meaning as the underlined part of the sentence. Two choices will not be used.

a. kind of like **b.** exactly like **c.** less like **d.** more like

1. Many animals take care of their young __________ people do.

2. This cake tastes __________ mom's, but it's not the same.

C. Fill in the blanks using the expressions from the box.

at different rates	similar to	the key to

1. My dog is very ____________________ yours. He barks all night when we are trying to sleep.
2. Our English skills are improving ____________________.
3. Hard work is ____________________ success.

Summary

D. Complete the summary with the correct words.

age	immortality	rates	infant	unique

Brooke Greenberg has a __________ aging condition. Only her hair and nails seem to grow normally, and all the other parts of her body age at different __________. She is 16 years old, but her body is still that of an __________. Scientists hope that her condition can teach us about how people __________. Some people even think she may be the key to __________.

Writing

E. Unscramble the words and write them in the blanks.

1. in the same way / do / Brooke does not / that other people / age

____.

2. scientists are / so different / trying to / discover what / makes Brooke

____.

3. better understand / Brooke will / age / help us / how people

____.

F. Read the question and arrange the words into a complete and correct answer.

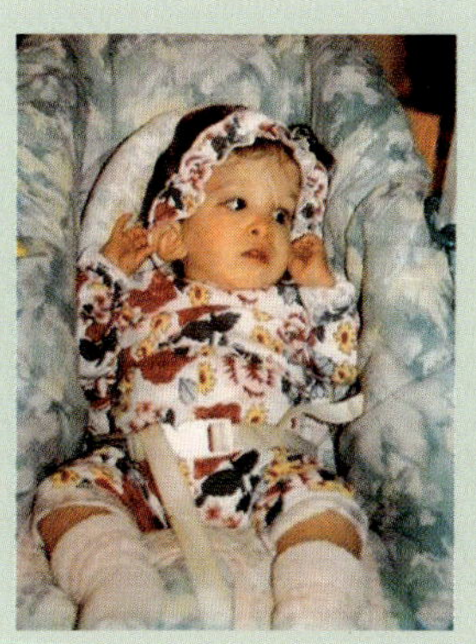

Q. What does this picture show?
(Brooke Greenberg / years / at / old / three)

➡ It shows ____
______________________________.

UNIT 10 A Daring Escape

Words & Expressions

A. Choose the correct definition for each word below.

missing	flight attendant	search	approach	hijacking

1. ________________ : when a criminal takes over a car, plane, or train
2. ________________ : a person who takes care of plane passengers
3. ________________ : to move towards a person or place
4. ________________ : unable to be found
5. ________________ : to look for

B. Choose the word that best completes each sentence.

1. The president's murder is an incredible ________ mystery.

   a. missing b. daring c. unsolved d. approaching

2. The plane will ________ soon. Please fasten your seatbelts.

   a. rush b. search c. escape d. land

3. There were 40 ________ on the bus when it crashed. Luckily everyone survived.

   a. hijackings b. passengers c. parachutes d. flights

C. Fill in the blanks using the expressions from the box.

in the air	to this day	up front

1. There is a strange smell ________________. I think something is wrong.
2. We thought he would come back, but ________________ no one has heard from him.
3. You can ride ________________. I don't mind riding in the back.

Summary

D. Complete the summary with the correct words.

parachutes	pilot	jumped	hijacked	seen

In 1971 a man who called himself Dan Cooper ____________ a plane flying over Portland, Oregon. He demanded $200,000 dollars and four ____________. Once he got what he wanted he ordered the ____________ to fly the plane back into the air. When they were in the air, he ____________ out of the plane with the money, and was never ____________ again.

Writing

E. Unscramble the words and write them in the blanks.

1. Dan Cooper / handed a note / a man / to a flight attendant / calling himself

____.

2. they discovered / the plane / open / and cold rain / the door / blowing into

____.

3. below / the FBI / for days / the ground / searched

____.

F. Read the question and arrange the words into a complete and correct answer.

Q. What is this a picture of?
(what / might / an FBI sketch / of / look like / Dan Cooper)

➡ It is ____
________________________.

UNIT 11 Sweet Disaster

Words & Expressions

A. Choose the correct definition for each word below.

form	drown	entire	gallon	slam

1. ________________ : a unit of liquid equaling about four liters

2. ________________ : to make into a shape

3. ________________ : to hit against with great force

4. ________________ : to die underwater from having no air

5. ________________ : whole

B. Choose the word that best completes each sentence.

1. We had five feet of water in our basement after the ________ .

a. flood **b.** mess **c.** track **d.** gallon

2. My brother makes a big ________ every time he eats.

a. track **b.** wave **c.** flood **d.** mess

3. Fred is ________ me because I cut down his tree.

a. slamming **b.** rushing **c.** lifting **d.** suing

C. Fill in the blanks using the expressions from the box.

in damages	needless to say	made of

1. Did you know that hot dogs and sausages are ________________ pig guts?

2. ________________ , Bill was very angry after the accident.

3. The judge awarded my grandmother $5,000 ________________ .

Summary

D. Complete the summary with the correct words.

lifting	knocking	rushed	sued	crushed

In 1919 a giant tank of molasses burst open in downtown Boston. Molasses ____________ into the streets at a speed of 35 miles per hour, ____________ over buildings, and even ____________ a train off of its tracks. Many people were ____________ to death and drowned. The people of Boston ____________ the molasses company and were given 6.6 million dollars in damages.

Writing

E. Unscramble the words and write them in the blanks.

1. 2.3 million gallons / of Boston / rushed / of molasses / into the streets

____.

2. the waist deep mess / many others / trapped in / drowned after / they were

____.

3. remembers / by the wave / being / he / picked up

____.

F. Read the question and arrange the words into a complete and correct answer.

Q. What does the picture show?
(molasses / a spoon / thick / from / dripping)

➡ It shows ________________________.

UNIT 12

Gone

Words & Expressions

A. Choose the correct definition for each word below.

block	extinction	rule	asteroid	dramatically

1. ________________ : happening in an extreme manner
2. ________________ : to prevent from reaching
3. ________________ : the death of every kind of a certain animal
4. ________________ : to control
5. ________________ : a giant rock traveling through space

B. Choose the word that best completes each sentence.

1. The nuclear explosion sent ________ all the way through the earth.

a. shock waves   b. extinctions   c. mega-tsunamis   d. volcanic eruptions

2. The Dodo went ________ because of disease and over-hunting.

a. extinct   b. dramatic   c. terrible   d. released

3. Cars ________ harmful gases into the air.

a. release   b. measure   c. block   d. rule

C. Fill in the blanks using the expressions from the box.

across the globe	any room for	figure out

1. I can't ________________ this math problem. Could you help me?
2. People ________________ were saddened by the death of Michael Jackson.
3. Is there ________________ me in that car?

Summary

D. Complete the summary with the correct words.

ash	impact	dead	asteroid	sunlight

Dinosaurs went extinct about 65 million years ago when a giant ____________ crashed into the earth. The ____________ started fires, earthquakes, volcanic eruptions and mega-tsunami. Dust and ____________ stayed in the air and blocked ____________ from reaching the earth. The earth cooled down, plants died, and eventually every dinosaur on Earth was completely ____________.

Writing

E. Unscramble the words and write them in the blanks.

1. ruled / over / the earth / for /160 million years / dinosaurs

____.

2. it sent / earthquakes / through / creating / shock waves / the earth,

____.

3. for years / the sun's light / dust and ash / in the sky / blocked

____.

F. Read the question and arrange the words into a complete and correct answer.

Q. What does the picture show?
(crashing / the earth / into / asteroid / an)

➡ It shows ______________________________.

UNIT 13 Zombie Ants!

Words & Expressions

A. Choose the correct definition for each word below.

the natural world	location	spore	the forest floor	zombie

1. ________________ : a creature that is controlled by something else
2. ________________ : the wild; where plants and animals live
3. ________________ : the place where something is
4. ________________ : what fungi use to reproduce
5. ________________ : the ground below groups of trees

B. Choose the word that best completes each sentence.

1. You need to ________ your dog. He looks dangerous.

   a. infect b. control c. reproduce d. provide

2. I think I was ________ with a strange virus this weekend.

   a. attached b. provided c. infected d. realized

3. I hope my rabbits ________ soon. Bunnies are so cute!

   a. provide b. realize c. terrify d. reproduce

C. Fill in the blanks using the expressions from the box.

soon after	close to	bite onto

1. Be careful with that turtle. It might ________________ your finger and not let go.
2. I left the house and ________________ Kevin called me.
3. I never knew that you lived so ________________ me.

Summary

D. Complete the summary with the correct words.

brains	infects	spores	climb	fungus

A special kind of ____________ infects only ants. It takes control of their ____________ and then kills them. But before the ants die, the fungus makes them ____________ up a certain plant and bite onto the underside of a leaf. The ant dies, and the fungus grows in its body. From under the leaf, it drops ____________ down to the ground below and ____________ more ants.

Writing

E. Unscramble the words and write them in the blanks.

1. keeps / attached / the dead body / to the leaf / its mouth

____.

2. a convenient way / this location / to reproduce / provides / for the fungus

____.

3. the forest floor / away from / carpenter ants / in the trees / live high

____.

F. Read the question and arrange the words into a complete and correct answer.

Q. What is shown in the picture?
(is / a dead / out of / growing / ant)

➡ The fungus ________________________________.

UNIT 14 Why Stripes?

Words & Expressions

A. Choose the correct definition for each word below.

still	color-blind	bite	temperature	spot

1. ________________ : to see something that is hard to see
2. ________________ : unable to see many different colors
3. ________________ : not moving
4. ________________ : to hold and squeeze with one's mouth
5. ________________ : how hot or cold a thing is

B. Choose the word that best completes each sentence.

1. Penguins are like humans because they ________ for life.

   a. reflect   b. control   c. mate   d. absorb

2. My pillow is covered in a red and white striped ________. I think it looks great.

   a. pattern   b. identification   c. temperature   d. predator

3. Babies often ________ their parents by their voices.

   a. control   b. spot   c. confuse   d. identify

C. Fill in the blanks using the expressions from the box.

mate with	for some reason	had a hard time

1. I want more bunnies, but my rabbits won't ________________ each other.
2. I ________________ finishing this project, but I think it turned out well.
3. I turned my heat on, but ________________ my floor is still cold.

Summary

D. Complete the summary with the correct words.

identification	mates	camouflage	unique	temperature

A zebra's stripes have many uses. They help ____________ the zebra from lions and also tsetse flies. They are useful for ____________, as each zebra's stripes are ____________. They might help the zebra control their body ____________, and they could even help zebras identify healthy ____________.

Writing

E. Unscramble the words and write them in the blanks.

1. when a zebra is / spotting it / in tall grass, / a lion has a hard time / standing still

____.

2. protect it / a zebra's / a tiny predator / stripes / from

____.

3. their white stripes / and their black stripes / reflect / absorb it / heat

____.

F. Read the question and arrange the words into a complete and correct answer.

Q. What does the picture show?
(pulling / four / carriage / zebras / a)

➡ It shows ________________________________

________________________________.

UNIT 15 Instead of Us

Words & Expressions

A. Choose the correct definition for each word below.

model	jewelry	explosion	subject	react

1. ________________ : metal and stone decorations worn by people
2. ________________ : a copy of an object that is used for display
3. ________________ : to respond to an action by doing something
4. ________________ : a sudden, violent burst of energy
5. ________________ : a person used for a science experiment

B. Choose the word that best completes each sentence.

1. That does not look like a comfortable ________ . Do you want to switch seats with me?

   a. CPR   b. mechanical lung   c. radiation   d. position

2. Do you think this cake will ________ for long if we put it in the fridge?

   a. display   b. detonate   c. react   d. last

3. Many people survived the explosion but died later from the ________ .

   a. models   b. radiation   c. Dutch   d. situation

C. Fill in the blanks using the expressions from the box.

out of the corner of my eye	turn around	full of

1. I know you are there. I can see you ________________ .
2. Don't ________________ now, but there is a wolf right behind you!
3. I want to swim in a pool ________________ noodles!

Summary

D. Complete the summary with the correct words.

accidents	smaller	CPR	models	rescue

Mannequins are usually used to display clothes, hats, and jewelry, but they have many other uses as well. The first mannequins were much _____________ . Artists used them as _____________ of the human body. _____________ workers use mannequins to practice _____________ . They also practice saving mannequins from _____________ and fires. Mannequins are also used as test subjects in nuclear explosions.

Writing

E. Unscramble the words and write them in the blanks.

1. out of / you see / the corner of / a person / your eye

____ .

2. on mannequins / mechanical lungs / practice CPR / rescue workers / with

____ .

3. to test / mannequins have / a nuclear explosion / react to / been used / how humans will

____ .

F. Read the question and arrange the words into a complete and correct answer.

Q. What does this picture show?
(as a model / that / a mannequin / artists / use)

➡ It shows _______________________________________ .

16 UNIT Stuck Together

Words & Expressions

A. Choose the correct definition for each word below.

replace	zipper	silent	space shuttle	button

1. ________________ : a small circular piece of plastic used to fasten clothes
2. ________________ : to take the place of
3. ________________ : a metal fastener used to close bags and jackets
4. ________________ : a vehicle used to transport astronauts through space
5. ________________ : not making any sound

B. Choose the word that best completes each sentence.

1. Here, help me ________ this rope to the tent.

a. scratch **b.** attach **c.** cover **d.** replace

2. I use a back ________ to help me get all those hard to reach places.

a. helmet **b.** patch **c.** pocket **d.** scratcher

3. These ________ show what military rank I am.

a. shoelaces **b.** pockets **c.** patches **d.** square inches

C. Fill in the blanks using the expressions from the box.

put on	thanks to	stick to

1. We won the election, and it is all ____________ the support of so many dedicated people.
2. Are you going to ____________ your hat, or are you just going to carry it in your hand?
3. Did you know that a balloon will ____________ the ceiling if you rub it on your head first?

Summary

D. Complete the summary with the correct words.

patches	silent	attaching	buttons	easier

Velcro has many incredible uses. Its inventor thought it would replace ____________ and zippers, but it has done more than that. It is used on space shuttles for ____________ tools and astronauts to walls. The army developed a ____________ version of Velcro for uniforms, ____________, and backpacks. Kids' clothing and shoes also use Velcro because it is ____________ than anything else.

Writing

E. Unscramble the words and write them in the blanks.

1. people have found / space / for Velcro / all over Earth, / incredible uses / and even in

____.

2. in each of / NASA uses / its space shuttles / over ten thousand / square inches of Velcro

____.

3. the Army uses / uniforms / for their patches / Velcro / on soldier's

____.

F. Read the question and arrange the words into a complete and correct answer.

Q. What does the picture show?
(on / hooks / a piece of / tiny / Velcro)

➡ It shows a close-up view of ____________________
____________________.

17
UNIT

A Self-Portrait?

Words & Expressions

A. Choose the correct definition for each word below.

actually	researcher	perfectly	self-portrait	compare

1. ________________ : done with no mistakes
2. ________________ : truly, really
3. ________________ : someone who looks for information
4. ________________ : to consider how two things are different and/or similar
5. ________________ : a portrait that an artist creates of himself or herself

B. Choose the word that best completes each sentence.

1. Do you know ________ we're having hamburgers or sandwiches for lunch?

a. in case **b.** whether **c.** although **d.** by the time

2. My sister looks older than me, but she is ________ younger than me.

a. perfectly **b.** mostly **c.** actually **d.** briefly

3. When we ________ the two rocks, we found that they were slightly different.

a. guessed **b.** hid **c.** borrowed **d.** compared

C. Fill in the blanks using the expressions from the box.

it is hard to tell	by the time	match up

1. Look at that person. ________________ whether they are a man or a woman.
2. These two puzzle pieces ________________ perfectly.
3. I will be rich ________________ I am 40 years old.

Summary

D. Complete the summary with the correct words.

model	self-portrait	mystery	painting	perfectly

The Mona Lisa isn't just a famous painting. It is a ____________ as well. Some people think it is actually a ____________ of the painter, Leonardo da Vinci. One researcher found that one of Leonardo's self-portraits matches up ____________ with the Mona Lisa. Others think Leonardo was actually ____________ his mother. They say it looks like a self-portrait because Leonardo used himself as a ____________ .

Writing

E. Unscramble the words and write them in the blanks.

1. researchers / the painting shows / have argued / and what / about who

____ .

2. sitting in / the painting / and looking outwards / a woman / shows / a chair

____ .

3. have great fun / these people / of the Mona Lisa's smile / guess the secret / trying to

____ .

F. Read the question and arrange the words into a complete and correct answer.

Q. What does the picture show?
(a famous painting / The Last Supper / called / by Leonardo da Vinci)

➡ It shows ______________________________
______________________________________ .

18 UNIT What Is Art?

Words & Expressions

A. Choose the correct definition for each word below.

fake	public	graffiti	artwork	price tag

1. ________________ : something that is considered to be art
2. ________________ : not real
3. ________________ : available to be used by anybody
4. ________________ : writing, painting, or drawing done on a public building
5. ________________ : a small sign attached to a thing showing how much it costs

B. Choose the word that best completes each sentence.

1. Daniel is a well-respected art ________. If he says that an artwork is good, its price goes up quickly.

   a. vandal b. critic c. price tag d. performance artist

2. I was ________ by the school lunch today. I think the meat was rotten.

   a. signed b. preserved c. arrested d. disgusted

3. The actors put on an amazing ________ last night. They should be proud.

   a. vandal b. performance c. graffiti d. sculpture

C. Fill in the blanks using the expressions from the box.

it's hard to argue with	pay for	filled with

1. In the morning, our school is ________________ kids.
2. Are you going to be able to ________________ that? It's very expensive.
3. I don't really need a new phone, but ________________ such a great deal.

Summary

D. Complete the summary with the correct words.

shark	public	$8 million	performance	Banksy

Modern art can take many forms. Damien Hirst preserved a dead ____________ in a glass box and called it art. He sold it for ____________. Graffiti artists spray-paint on ____________ buildings. This is illegal, but one graffiti artist, named ____________, is allowed to do it just because his art is so popular. ____________ artists don't just make art, they do it. They put on special art performances in public places.

Writing

E. Unscramble the words and write them in the blanks.

1. it was a men's urinal / with a fake name / that he turned / and signed / upside down

____.

2. "art" was / of what / embraced / the art world / his new idea

____.

3. spray-painting on / anyone caught / arrested or fined / a public building / is usually

____.

F. Read the question and arrange the words into a complete and correct answer.

Q. What does the picture show?
(colorful / a house / on / graffiti / in Brazil)

➡ It shows ______________________________
______________________.

19
UNIT

Human Lightning Rod

Words & Expressions

A. Choose the correct definition for each word below.

chance	flee	steal	eyebrows	strike

1. ____________________ : to run away
2. ____________________ : to take something which isn't yours
3. ____________________ : hair on your forehead above your eyes
4. ____________________ : to hit with great force
5. ____________________ : the possibility that a thing will happen

B. Choose the word that best completes each sentence.

1. If you are ever lost in the woods, a(n) __________ would be able to save you.

   a. lightning bolt b. billionaire c. eyebrow d. park ranger

2. The army has __________ that can travel both on land and in water.

   a. sticks b. thunderstorms c. lotteries d. vehicles

3. I __________ the coffee slowly so I wouldn't spill it.

   a. poured b. struck c. occurred d. fled

C. Fill in the blanks using the expressions from the box.

left a hole	paid off	at all times

1. Following your advice really ____________________. I made $3,000 just last week!
2. When you are hiking you should keep a map with you ____________________.
3. The bullet went through my body and ____________________ in my shoulder.

Summary

D. Complete the summary with the correct words.

fifth	seven	park ranger	water	cursed

Roy Sullivan was struck by lightning ____________ times during his life. After the first four strikes he began to believe he was ____________ . He kept a can of ____________ with him at all times. The ____________ time he was struck, his hair caught on fire and he put it out with the can of water. All of the strikes occurred while Ray worked as a ____________ at Shenandoah National Park.

Writing

E. Unscramble the words and write them in the blanks.

1. 1/6,000 / the chance / struck / of being / once in your life / is

____ .

2. the lightning bolt / a hole / burned a strip / and left / down his right leg / in his shoe

____ .

3. over his head / the can of / he just grabbed / water / and poured it

____ .

F. Read the question and arrange the words into a complete and correct answer.

Q. What does the picture show?
(city / strike / a big / a lightning / over)

➡ It shows ______________________________________
______________________ .

UNIT 20

A Shocking Sight

Words & Expressions

A. Choose the correct definition for each word below.

expect	tingle	pew	miniature	incredible

1. ________________ : amazing
2. ________________ : smaller than normal
3. ________________ : a long wooden seat with a back
4. ________________ : to think that something will happen
5. ________________ : to feel strange and a little ticklish

B. Choose the word that best completes each sentence.

1. Nobody has a(n) ________ for this mess? Then all of you will be punished.

   a. explanation b. bang c. phenomenon d. hoax

2. I can't believe you think that dinosaurs never ________!

   a. struck b. existed c. floated d. destroyed

3. If you're not careful, that experiment might ________ and hurt you.

   a. explode b. tingle c. exist d. float

C. Fill in the blanks using the expressions from the box.

smelled badly	other times	close by

1. After falling in the pond, Bill ________________ of rotten vegetables.
2. You live ________________, don't you? Do you want me to walk you home?
3. Sometimes I like spinach, but ________________ it tastes disgusting.

Summary

D. Complete the summary with the correct words.

miniature	hoax	damaged	visions	lightning

Ball lightning is a slow moving, ball-shaped type of lightning. Scientists used to think that it was just a ____________ or a fantasy, but now they think it is real. In 1638 ball lightning ____________ the inside of a church. Other times it has struck people and killed them. Some scientists think ball lightning may actually be ____________ black holes. Others think ball lightning might just be strange ____________ caused by regular ____________.

Writing

E. Unscramble the words and write them in the blanks.

1. a rare, slow-moving, / there have been / stories of / of lightning / ball-shaped kind

____.

2. one of / comes / the earliest stories / from 1638 / of ball lightning

____.

3. to think / can cause us / floating circles / a close strike of lightning / that we are seeing

____.

F. Read the question and arrange the words into a complete and correct answer.

Q. What does the picture show?
(made / being / a microwave / in / ball lightning)

➡ It shows ____
____________________.

Notes

Notes

Notes

Reading Highlights

Reading Highlights is a three-book reading comprehension series for intermediate learners of English as a foreign language. Intriguing and stimulating content is delivered through a series of approachable and well-organized passages. The clarity and natural feel of the writing encourages students to engage the text with an inquisitive mind. Students are guided towards the discovery that written English can be fun and relevant to their lives and interests.

Key Features:

- Colorful and Engaging graphics that present the material in an eye-catching way
- Vocabulary exercises that lead students from reviewing the unit vocabulary to practicing and expanding their use of it
- Comprehension exercises that test understanding and encourage an investigative approach to reading
- Organize exercises that provide a framework for students to re-state and re-organize passage content
- Synthesize exercises that help students recall passage content in a new way

Components

- Student Book / Workbook

Download resources at **www.wcbooks.co.kr**
MP3 files / Word lists / Translations with answer keys / Test sheets

Reading Highlights Series

WorldCom Edu www.wcbooks.co.kr